The
TIME FOR PRAYER
Program

זְמַן לִתְפִילָה

BOOK 4: תּוֹרָה
Dina Maiben and Hillary Zana

A.R.E. Publishing, Inc.

Denver, Colorado

INTRODUCTION

Imagine that you are standing at the foot of Mount Sinai as Moses brings down the Ten Commandments. Thunder and lightning fill the air, and every heart beats with anticipation and excitement. The Kabbalists (Jewish mystics) teach that the Torah service reenacts the receiving of the Torah at Mount Sinai. Here's how it works.

Match the people and steps involved in the Torah service with those from Mount Sinai.

_____ 1. In some communities, an officer (גַּבַּאי) chooses members of the congregation for Torah honors.

_____ 2. The Torah is kept in the Ark (אֲרוֹן הַקֹּדֶשׁ).

_____ 3. When the Torah is taken from the Ark, the congregation recites the שְׁמַע.

_____ 4. The ceremony takes place on a raised platform (בִּימָה).

_____ 5. The Torah is carried into the congregation.

_____ 6. Individuals come up to recite the blessings (עֲלִיָּה).

_____ 7. The Cantor or other designated individual (בַּעַל-קְרִיאָה) reads the Torah.

ת. The Ten Commandments are given on top of Mount Sinai (הַר סִינַי).

שׁ. God selects Israel to receive the Torah.

ר. Moses carries the two tablets (לוּחוֹת) down to the Israelite camp.

מ. מֹשֶׁה reads the Ten Commandments to the Israelites.

ח. The Israelites call out שְׁמַע יִשְׂרָאֵל when מֹשֶׁה comes near.

ו. The two לוּחוֹת are carried in the Ark of the Covenant.

ה. The Torah belongs to every individual Jew.

The Torah is written without vowels. Using the number code, fill in the letters to find the name of the Torah's special holiday.

___	___	___	___	___	___	___	___
6	5	2	4	4	3	7	1

CHAPTER 1

"We Give Honor to the Torah."

סֵדֶר הוֹצָאַת הַתּוֹרָה

Complete each Hebrew label using the words from the word box below.

WORD BOX

בִּימָה

פָּרֹכֶת

נֵר תָּמִיד

סֵפֶר תּוֹרָה

אֲרוֹן הַקֹּדֶשׁ

Literally, the "Always Candle," this lamp burns constantly.

_____

Literally, "The Holy Ark," this cabinet houses the Torah scrolls.

_____

A Torah scroll — literally, "Book of Torah"

_____

A curtain in the Ark. While the Israelites wandered in the Sinai, a curtain of purple, blue, and crimson yarns and fine linen kept the Ark from sight.

_____

Literally, "stage," this is the raised platform from which the service is led.

_____

רִמּוֹן

חֹשֶׁן

עֵץ חַיִּים

The Torah holds the central place in the sanctuary because of what's in it.

What's in the Torah?

Fill in the blanks with the Hebrew words that best match each student's English answer. Then write your own answer in the space provided.

WORD BOX

שַׁבָּת וְיוֹם טוֹב   אֶרֶץ יִשְׂרָאֵל   אַבְרָהָם וְשָׂרָה
מִצְוֹת   עִבְרִית   פֶּסַח
צְדָקָה   שָׁלוֹם

There are 304,805 Hebrew letters, but no vowels in the Torah!

_____

The Torah reminds us about the Land of Israel, and why it belongs to the Jewish people.

_____

The Torah is filled with laws. It's just like that dream I once had.

_____

The Torah teaches us to treat other people with justice.

_____

The Torah is a link to our past. It tells about our Exodus from Egypt.

_____

The Torah tells the stories of our ancestors.

_____

The Torah holds our hopes for the future.

_____

My grandpa taught me that we study the Torah to learn about Jewish traditions and celebrations.

_____

אֲנִי

_____
_____

The Torah is taken from the אֲרוֹן הַקֹּדֶשׁ in an elaborate ceremony.

The Twelve Gates

There are twelve gates through which the prayers of Israel ascend into heaven. Each tradition has its own gate. Thus, each Israelite should pray according to his or her own tradition so as not to bring confusion into the higher realms. (Rabbi Isaac Luria, 1534-1572)

Liberal Version

There is none like You among the gods, Eternal One,	אֵין כָּמֽוֹךָ בָאֱלֹהִים אֲדֹנָי, .1
and there is nothing like Your creations.	וְאֵין כְּמַעֲשֶׂיךָ. .2
Your reign is everlasting,	מַלְכוּתְךָ מַלְכוּת כָּל־עוֹלָמִים, .3
and Your sovereignty is from generation to generation.	וּמֶמְשַׁלְתְּךָ בְּכָל־דּוֹר וָדוֹר. .4
Adonai is Ruler, Adonai has always been Ruler,	יְיָ מֶֽלֶךְ, יְיָ מָלָךְ, .5
Adonai will rule forever.	יְיָ יִמְלֹךְ לְעוֹלָם וָעֶד. .6
The Eternal will grant strength to our people,	יְיָ עֹז לְעַמּוֹ יִתֵּן, .7
The Eternal will bless our people with peace.	יְיָ יְבָרֵךְ אֶת־עַמּוֹ בַשָּׁלוֹם. .8
Source of mercy, may You improve Zion	אֵל הָרַחֲמִים, הֵיטִֽיבָה בִרְצוֹנְךָ אֶת־צִיּוֹן .9
may You rebuild the walls of Jerusalem.	תִּבְנֶה חוֹמוֹת יְרוּשָׁלָֽיִם. .10
For in You alone do we trust, Sovereign God,	כִּי בְךָ לְבַד בָּטָֽחְנוּ, .11
high and exalted, Ruler of all the worlds.	מֶֽלֶךְ אֵל רָם וְנִשָּׂא, אֲדוֹן עוֹלָמִים. .12
Magnify God, and give honor to the Torah.	הָבוּ גֹֽדֶל לֵאלֹהֵֽינוּ וּתְנוּ כָבוֹד לַתּוֹרָה. א.13
For the Torah shall go forth from Zion,	כִּי מִצִּיּוֹן תֵּצֵא תוֹרָה, .14
and the word of the Eternal from Jerusalem.	וּדְבַר יְיָ מִירוּשָׁלָֽיִם. .15
Blessed is the One Who gave the Torah	בָּרוּךְ שֶׁנָּתַן תּוֹרָה, .16
to our people, Israel, in sanctity.	לְעַמּוֹ יִשְׂרָאֵל בִּקְדֻשָּׁתוֹ. .17
House of Jacob, come let us walk by God's light.	בֵּית יַעֲקֹב, לְכוּ וְנֵלְכָה בְּאוֹר יְיָ. א.17
Listen Israel: Adonai our God is One.	שְׁמַע יִשְׂרָאֵל יְיָ אֱלֹהֵֽינוּ יְיָ אֶחָד. .18
God is one and great, holy is God's name.	אֶחָד אֱלֹהֵֽינוּ, גָּדוֹל אֲדוֹנֵֽינוּ, קָדוֹשׁ שְׁמוֹ. .19
Magnify God with me, as we exalt God's name.	גַּדְּלוּ לַיְיָ אִתִּי, וּנְרוֹמְמָה שְׁמוֹ יַחְדָּו. .20
To You, Eternal One, is the greatness, and the power,	לְךָ, יְיָ, הַגְּדֻלָּה וְהַגְּבוּרָה .21
the glory, the victory, and the majesty:	וְהַתִּפְאֶֽרֶת וְהַנֵּֽצַח וְהַהוֹד, .22
for all that is in heaven and earth is Yours.	כִּי כֹל בַּשָּׁמַֽיִם וּבָאָֽרֶץ, .23
Yours is the realm	לְךָ יְיָ הַמַּמְלָכָה .24
Yours is the supreme sovereignty.	וְהַמִּתְנַשֵּׂא לְכֹל לְרֹאשׁ. .25

☐ = added in Traditional versions   = added in some Liberal versions

There is none like You among the gods, Eternal One,	אֵין כָּמוֹךָ בָאֱלֹהִים אֲדֹנָי, .1
and there is nothing like Your creations.	וְאֵין כְּמַעֲשֶׂיךָ. .2
Your reign is everlasting,	מַלְכוּתְךָ מַלְכוּת כָּל־עוֹלָמִים, .3
and Your sovereignty is from generation to generation.	וּמֶמְשַׁלְתְּךָ בְּכָל־דּוֹר וָדוֹר. .4
Adonai is Ruler, Adonai has always been Ruler,	יְיָ מֶלֶךְ, יְיָ מָלָךְ, .5
Adonai will rule forever.	יְיָ יִמְלֹךְ לְעֹלָם וָעֶד. .6
The Eternal will grant strength to our people,	יְיָ עֹז לְעַמּוֹ יִתֵּן, .7
The Eternal will bless our people with peace.	יְיָ יְבָרֵךְ אֶת־עַמּוֹ בַשָּׁלוֹם. .8
Source of mercy, may You improve Zion	אַב הָרַחֲמִים, הֵיטִיבָה בִרְצוֹנְךָ אֶת־צִיּוֹן .9
may You rebuild the walls of Jerusalem.	תִּבְנֶה חוֹמוֹת יְרוּשָׁלָיִם. .10
For in You alone do we trust, Sovereign God,	כִּי בְךָ לְבַד בָּטָחְנוּ, .11
high and exalted, Ruler of all the worlds.	מֶלֶךְ אֵל רָם וְנִשָּׂא, אֲדוֹן עוֹלָמִים. .12

When the Ark was carried forward, Moses said:	וַיְהִי בִּנְסֹעַ הָאָרֹן וַיֹּאמֶר מֹשֶׁה: .13ב
"Arise Eternal One, and scatter Your foes,	קוּמָה יְיָ וְיָפֻצוּ אֹיְבֶיךָ, .13ג
and drive Your enemies from before You."	וְיָנֻסוּ מְשַׂנְאֶיךָ מִפָּנֶיךָ. .13ד

For the Torah shall go forth from Zion,	כִּי מִצִּיּוֹן תֵּצֵא תוֹרָה, .14
and the word of the Eternal from Jerusalem.	וּדְבַר יְיָ מִירוּשָׁלָיִם. .15
Blessed is the One Who gave the Torah	בָּרוּךְ שֶׁנָּתַן תּוֹרָה, .16
to our people, Israel, in sanctity.	לְעַמּוֹ יִשְׂרָאֵל בִּקְדֻשָּׁתוֹ. .17

(Various meditations may be added here.)

Listen Israel: Adonai our God is One.	שְׁמַע יִשְׂרָאֵל יְיָ אֱלֹהֵינוּ יְיָ אֶחָד. .18
God is one and great, holy is God's name.	אֶחָד אֱלֹהֵינוּ, גָּדוֹל אֲדוֹנֵינוּ, קָדוֹשׁ שְׁמוֹ. .19
Magnify God with me, as we exalt God's name.	גַּדְּלוּ לַיְיָ אִתִּי, וּנְרוֹמְמָה שְׁמוֹ יַחְדָּו. .20
To You, Eternal One, is the greatness, and the power,	לְךָ, יְיָ, הַגְּדֻלָּה וְהַגְּבוּרָה .21
the glory, the victory, and the majesty:	וְהַתִּפְאֶרֶת וְהַנֵּצַח וְהַהוֹד, .22
for all that is in heaven and earth is Yours.	כִּי כֹל בַּשָּׁמַיִם וּבָאָרֶץ, .23
Yours is the realm	לְךָ יְיָ הַמַּמְלָכָה .24
Yours is the supreme sovereignty.	וְהַמִּתְנַשֵּׂא לְכֹל לְרֹאשׁ. .25

Exalt the Eternal our God, and bow low	רוֹמְמוּ יְיָ אֱלֹהֵינוּ וְהִשְׁתַּחֲווּ לַהֲדֹם רַגְלָיו, .26
to God's footstool, God is sacred.	קָדוֹשׁ הוּא. .27
Exalt the Eternal our God and bow low	רוֹמְמוּ יְיָ אֱלֹהֵינוּ וְהִשְׁתַּחֲווּ לְהַר קָדְשׁוֹ .28
to God's holy mountain, for our God is sanctified.	כִּי קָדוֹשׁ יְיָ אֱלֹהֵינוּ. .29

Prayerobics

In Ashkenazi congregations, the Cantor recites the שְׁמַע when the Torah is removed from the Ark. This is followed by the line that begins אֶחָד אֱלֹהֵינוּ. In Traditional congregations, the Cantor recites the lines first, and the congregation repeats them. In most Reform congregations, the lines are recited in unison. These two lines are followed by a third line:

גַּדְּלוּ לַיְיָ אִתִּי, וּנְרוֹמְמָה שְׁמוֹ יַחְדָּו.

In some congregations, everyone faces the Ark and bows when this line is chanted as a way to show honor for all the Torah scrolls.

Practice reciting these three lines the way they are recited in your congregation.

שְׁמַע יִשְׂרָאֵל יְיָ אֱלֹהֵינוּ יְיָ אֶחָד.
אֶחָד אֱלֹהֵינוּ, גָּדוֹל אֲדוֹנֵינוּ, קָדוֹשׁ שְׁמוֹ.
גַּדְּלוּ לַיְיָ אִתִּי, וּנְרוֹמְמָה שְׁמוֹ יַחְדָּו.

When the Torah is carried through the congregation, many people will touch the scroll with a Siddur, the corner of a tallit, or their fingers and then kiss what touched the Torah. In some Sephardic congregations, people wave at the Torah or open their arms as if to hug the scroll.

Find the words אֶחָד and גָּדוֹל in the prayer above. Both of these words are adjectives. Now look at one of the ways Hebrew deals with adjectives.

Language Enrichment

יֶלֶד גָּדוֹל
יַלְדָּה גְּדוֹלָה
יַלְדָּה קְטַנָּה
יֶלֶד קָטָן

Mrs. Shapiro's students posed for a picture with their little brothers and sisters.
Complete the sentences with the correct adjective in its correct form.

יְהוֹשֻׁעַ יֶלֶד _____.	דָּנִיֵּאל יֶלֶד _____. 1.
אֶסְתֵּר יַלְדָּה _____.	תָּמִי יַלְדָּה _____. 2.
אֵיתָן יֶלֶד _____.	רִבְקָה יַלְדָּה _____. 3.
יוֹסִי יֶלֶד _____.	בִּנְיָמִין יֶלֶד _____. 4.
אָדָם יֶלֶד _____.	שָׂרָה יַלְדָּה _____. 5.

Circle the correct adjective.

גְּדוֹלָה	גָּדוֹל	קְטַנָּה	קָטָן	הָאָח שֶׁל רִבְקָה... א.
גְּדוֹלָה	גָּדוֹל	קְטַנָּה	קָטָן	הָאָחוֹת שֶׁל תָּמִי... ב.
גְּדוֹלָה	גָּדוֹל	קְטַנָּה	קָטָן	הָאָח שֶׁל בִּנְיָמִין... ג.
גְּדוֹלָה	גָּדוֹל	קְטַנָּה	קָטָן	הָאָחוֹת שֶׁל אֶסְתֵּר... ד.

good (masc. sing.) = טוֹב	
good (fem. sing.) = טוֹבָה	
handsome (masc. sing.) = יָפֶה	
beautiful (fem. sing.) = יָפָה	

אוֹצַר מִלִּים
A TREASURY OF WORDS

Check כֵּן for each item that you see in the picture above, and לֹא for each item that is missing.

כֵּן	לֹא	
☐	☐	1. יֵשׁ סֻכָּה יָפָה עַל־יַד הָעֵץ.
☐	☐	2. יֵשׁ לְאֵיתָן טַלִּית קְטַנָּה.
☐	☐	3. יֵשׁ בִּימָה יָפָה בְּבֵית־הַכְּנֶסֶת.
☐	☐	4. יֵשׁ כֶּתֶר גָּדוֹל עַל סֵפֶר הַתּוֹרָה.
☐	☐	5. יֵשׁ לַחַזָּן כֶּלֶב טוֹב.
☐	☐	6. מוֹרָה טוֹבָה מִתְפַּלֶּלֶת בְּבֵית־הַכְּנֶסֶת.
☐	☐	7. יֵשׁ לְאָדָם כִּפָּה גְּדוֹלָה.
☐	☐	8. יֵשׁ חֹשֶׁן יָפֶה עַל סֵפֶר הַתּוֹרָה.
☐	☐	9. יֵשׁ פָּרֹכֶת יָפָה עַל אֲרוֹן הַקֹּדֶשׁ.
☐	☐	10. יֵשׁ דָּג גָּדוֹל בַּמַּיִם.
☐	☐	11. יֵשׁ רִמּוֹן קָטָן עַל עֵץ חַיִּים.

The Torah is our most precious possession. Now that your Hebrew skills are sharp,

it's time for you to begin learning how to read from the Torah.

כֶּתֶר תּוֹרָה

According to the Talmud. the Torah must be written in a special square script called כְּתָב אַשּׁוּרִי. In this script, many letters are written with crowns. Circle all the letters that have three crowns.

א ב ג ד ה ו ז ח ט י כ ך ל מ ם נ ן ס ע פ ף צ ץ ק ר ש ת

The Hebrew words below have all been written in Torah script without vowels. Match each Hebrew word to its picture. (Hint: If you need help, look back to pages 4, 9, and 10.)

חַזָּן

חֹדֶשׁ

קָטֹן

גָּדוֹל

כֶּתֶר

יִשְׂרָאֵל

רִמּוֹנִים

נֵר תָּמִיד

עֵץ חַיִּים

אֲרוֹן הַקֹּדֶשׁ

Many of our most important prayers can be found in the Torah. Practice reading this prayer, first with vowels, and then the way it is found in the Torah.

שְׁמַע יִשְׂרָאֵל יְיָ אֱלֹהֵינוּ, יְיָ אֶחָד.

שמע ישראל יהוה אלהינו יהוה אחד

The Torah has been taken from the Ark, paraded through the congregation, and opened — ready for reading. But before it can be read, the Torah Blessings must be recited. You will learn them in the next chapter.

KEY WORD:
תּוֹרָה

Reading Reminder

כָּל = כּוֹל

Practice reading these words and phrases.

1. בָּרְכוּ   מִכָּל   נָטַע   אֱמֶת   אֲשֶׁר

2. וְחַיֵי   הַמְבֹרָךְ   תּוֹרַת   תּוֹרָתוֹ   הָעַמִּים

3. לָנוּ   בָּנוּ   נָתַן   בָּחַר   בְּתוֹכֵנוּ

4. בָּחַר בָּנוּ   וְנָתַן לָנוּ   בְּתוֹכֵנוּ   אֶת־תּוֹרָתוֹ   מִכָּל־הָעַמִּים

5. אֲשֶׁר נָתַן לָנוּ תּוֹרַת אֱמֶת

6. בָּרוּךְ יְיָ הַמְבֹרָךְ לְעוֹלָם וָעֶד

7. וְחַיֵי עוֹלָם נָטַע בְּתוֹכֵנוּ

YIDBIT

The Rabbis began to formalize the synagogue service in the third century C.E. The practice of reading the Torah on Shabbat, Festivals, Mondays, and Thursdays was already centuries old by then. The tradition of calling עֲלִיּוֹת to the Torah dates back to the time of Ezra the Scribe. The number of עֲלִיּוֹת is based on the importance of the day.

שַׁבָּת	7
יוֹם כִּפּוּר	6
חַגִּים	5
New Jewish month and intermediate days of Festivals	4
Monday or Thursday	3

The Torah is our heritage, our destiny, and our gift to the world. Here is how we bless and honor it.

CHAPTER 2

בִּרְכוֹת הַתּוֹרָה

Blessing before the Torah reading

Praise Adonai, Who is blessed.	בָּרְכוּ אֶת־יְיָ הַמְבֹרָךְ. .1
Praised be Adonai Who is blessed, forever.	בָּרוּךְ יְיָ הַמְבֹרָךְ לְעוֹלָם וָעֶד. .2
Blessed are You Adonai our God,	בָּרוּךְ אַתָּה יְיָ אֱלֹהֵינוּ, .3
Sovereign of the universe	מֶלֶךְ הָעוֹלָם, .4
Who has chosen us from all peoples	אֲשֶׁר בָּחַר בָּנוּ מִכָּל־הָעַמִּים .5
and given us Your Torah.	וְנָתַן לָנוּ אֶת־תּוֹרָתוֹ. .6
Blessed are You Adonai, Giver of the Torah.	בָּרוּךְ אַתָּה יְיָ, נוֹתֵן הַתּוֹרָה. .7

Blessing after the Torah reading

Blessed are You Adonai our God,	בָּרוּךְ אַתָּה יְיָ אֱלֹהֵינוּ, .8
Sovereign of the universe,	מֶלֶךְ הָעוֹלָם, .9
Who has given us a Torah of truth,	אֲשֶׁר נָתַן לָנוּ תּוֹרַת אֱמֶת .10
and implanted eternal life within us.	וְחַיֵּי עוֹלָם נָטַע בְּתוֹכֵנוּ. .11
Blessed are You Adonai, Giver of the Torah.	בָּרוּךְ אַתָּה יְיָ, נוֹתֵן הַתּוֹרָה. .12

NOTE: Sephardic Jews recite the following passage before reading the Torah, while Ashkenazic Jews recite it after reading the Torah

This is the Torah that Moses placed	וְזֹאת הַתּוֹרָה אֲשֶׁר שָׂם מֹשֶׁה .13
before the Children of Israel	לִפְנֵי בְּנֵי יִשְׂרָאֵל .14
from the mouth of God and the hand of Moses.	עַל פִּי יְיָ בְּיַד מֹשֶׁה. .15

How many words are found in the Torah blessings without the בָּרְכוּ (lines 3-12)? _____ This is the number of days Moses spent on Sinai when he went up to get the Ten Commandments. Here are some other "magic" Torah numbers.

תּוֹרָה! תּוֹרָה! תּוֹרָה!

**The Torah is our most precious possession. Fill in the words and numbers from
the box on the right to learn six things you might not know about it.**

WORD BOX

5

לְמִשְׁפְּחֹתֵיהֶם

304,805

קְלָף

613

Computer scanning

79,976

gold

1. The Torah has: _____ Books   5,845 Verses

      54 Portions   _____ Words

      187 Chapters   _____ Letters

     _____ Commandments

2. Although there are no rules about the number of columns or sheets of
parchment that a סֵפֶר תּוֹרָה must have, a standard pattern of 248 columns
with 42 lines each has been in use since the beginning of the 1800s. Each
column must be wide enough to write לְמִשְׁפְּחֹתֵיהֶם (the longest word in the
Torah) three times in a row. Try it for yourself.

_____   _____   _____

3. A סֵפֶר תּוֹרָה must be written by hand, and the סוֹפֵר (scribe) must read
each word out loud before writing it. The Torah is written on _____
(parchment), not paper. קְלָף is made from the skins of kosher animals.
Special ink is also used.

4. No base metals (iron, steel, copper, brass, or bronze) may be used in
making, decorating, or repairing a סֵפֶר תּוֹרָה. Base metals are used to make
weapons, and nothing used to kill can be used to make a Torah scroll. Silver or
_____ needles are used to stitch the parchment sections together. Metal
pens are not used. Originally, pens were made from papyrus reeds. Today, most
scribes use quill pens made from goose or turkey feathers.

5. Many people believe that the סוֹפֵר is not allowed to make a mistake, but that
isn't true. The סוֹפֵר is allowed to correct a mistake in any word except God's name.

6. In ancient times, three correct copies of the Torah were kept in the Temple in
Jerusalem. Scribes had to check each new סֵפֶר תּוֹרָה against those three scrolls.
Today, three Rabbis check each new סֵפֶר תּוֹרָה to make sure that it is correct.
_____ _____ can now help with this job.

The Torah is so precious that we raise it up for all to see and dress it in finery.

Prayerobics

In Ashkenazic congregations, the Torah is lifted up after it is read. This is called הַגְבָּהָה, and the person who lifts it is called מַגְבִּיהַ. In Sephardic congregations, this ceremony is called הֲקָמָה, and it takes place before the Torah is read. In every congregation, the person who lifts the Torah opens it to show the congregation part of at least three columns. Some people point to the raised scroll with their index fingers, or point with the צִיצִת from the corner of a טַלִּית. The following line is recited when the Torah is lifted:

וְזֹאת הַתּוֹרָה אֲשֶׁר שָׂם מֹשֶׁה לִפְנֵי בְּנֵי יִשְׂרָאֵל עַל פִּי יְיָ בְּיַד מֹשֶׁה.

In Ashkenazic congregations, another individual is called up to roll and dress the Torah. This honor is called גְּלִילָה ("rolling"), and the person is called the גּוֹלֵל or גּוֹלֶלֶת. In Sephardic congregations, גְּלִילָה is done by one of the people already on the בִּימָה.

There are also customary ways to greet someone who has just had an עֲלִיָּה or other Torah honor. Ashkenazic Jews say: יִישַׁר כֹּחֲךָ or יִישַׁר כֹּחַ to a man and יִישַׁר כֹּחֵךְ to a woman. Sephardic Jews say: בָּרוּךְ וּבָרוּךְ. In both congregations, the response is: חֲזַק תִּהְיֶה or חֲזַק וֶאֱמָץ.

Fill in the blanks with the correct greetings.

חֲזַק וּבָרוּךְ

יִישַׁר כֹּחַ

On the day of your Bar or Bat Mitzvah, people will greet you in this wonderful way after you read your פָּרָשָׁה (Torah portion). You may also teach the congregation about your פָּרָשָׁה, so take a moment to learn more about it.

אוֹצַר מִלִּים
A TREASURY OF WORDS

עֲשֶׂרֶת הַדִּבְּרוֹת

יוֹם-הֻלֶּדֶת

Torah portion = פָּרָשָׁה
story = סִפּוּר
from = מִ_____

קוֹרֵא

קוֹרֵאת

The chart below shows the Hebrew for the five books of the תּוֹרָה, the twelve months of the Jewish calendar, and the four seasons. Use the chart to help Mrs. Shapiro's students complete their statements on the next page.

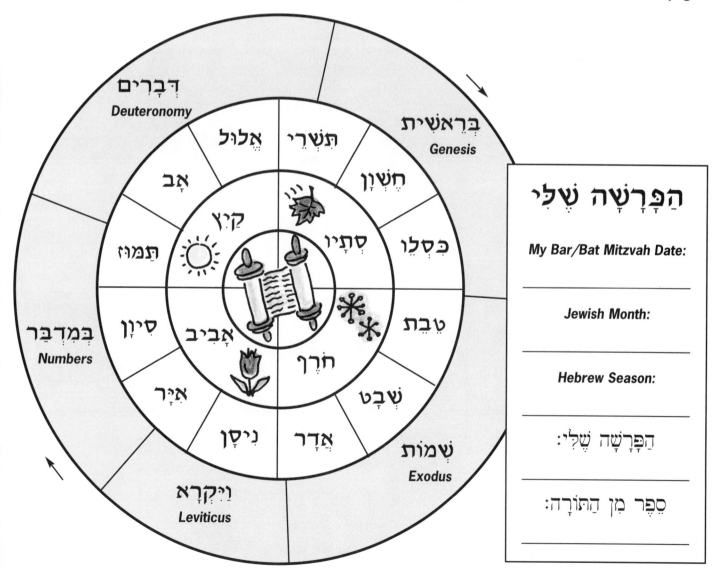

דְּבָרִים
Deuteronomy

בְּרֵאשִׁית
Genesis

אֱלוּל

תִּשְׁרֵי

חֶשְׁוָן

אָב

קַיִץ

כִּסְלֵו

תַּמּוּז

סְתָיו

בְּמִדְבַּר
Numbers

סִיוָן

אָבִיב

טֵבֵת

אִיָּר

חֹרֶף

שְׁבָט

נִיסָן

אֲדָר

שְׁמוֹת
Exodus

וַיִּקְרָא
Leviticus

הַפָּרָשָׁה שֶׁלִּי

My Bar/Bat Mitzvah Date:

_____

Jewish Month:

_____

Hebrew Season:

_____

הַפָּרָשָׁה שֶׁלִּי:

_____

סֵפֶר מִן הַתּוֹרָה:

_____

קְרִיאַת הַתּוֹרָה

יוֹם-הַהֻלֶּדֶת שֶׁלִּי בַּסְתָיו. בַּר הַמִּצְוָה שֶׁלִּי בְּחֹדֶשׁ תִּשְׁרֵי.
אֲנִי קוֹרֵא אֶת פָּרָשַׁת בְּרֵאשִׁית.
הַסִּפּוּר שֶׁל אָדָם וְחַוָּה בְּפָרָשַׁת בְּרֵאשִׁית.
הַפָּרָשָׁה שֶׁלִּי מִסְפֵּר _____.

יוֹם-הַהֻלֶּדֶת שֶׁלִּי בַּחֹרֶף. בַּת הַמִּצְוָה שֶׁלִּי בְּחֹדֶשׁ שְׁבָט.
אֲנִי קוֹרֵאת אֶת פָּרָשַׁת בֹּא.
הַסִּפּוּר שֶׁל מֹשֶׁה, מִרְיָם, וְחַג הַפֶּסַח בְּפָרָשַׁת בֹּא.
הַפָּרָשָׁה שֶׁלִּי מִסְפֵּר _____.

יוֹם-הַהֻלֶּדֶת שֶׁלִּי בַּקַּיִץ. בַּר הַמִּצְוָה שֶׁלִּי בְּחֹדֶשׁ תַּמּוּז.
אֲנִי _____ אֶת פָּרָשַׁת בָּלָק.
הַסִּפּוּר שֶׁל בִּלְעָם וְהַמֶּלֶךְ בָּלָק בְּפָרָשַׁת בָּלָק.
הַפָּרָשָׁה שֶׁלִּי מִסְפֵּר _____.

יוֹם-הַהֻלֶּדֶת שֶׁלִּי בָּאָבִיב. בַּת הַמִּצְוָה שֶׁלִּי בְּחֹדֶשׁ אִיָּר.
אֲנִי _____ אֶת פָּרָשַׁת קְדוֹשִׁים.
מִצְווֹת, חֻקִּים, וּמִשְׁפָּטִים בְּפָרָשַׁת קְדוֹשִׁים.
הַפָּרָשָׁה שֶׁלִּי מִסְפֵּר _____.

יוֹם-הַהֻלֶּדֶת שֶׁלִּי בַּ_____. בַּר הַמִּצְוָה שֶׁלִּי בְּחֹדֶשׁ אָב.
אֲנִי _____ אֶת פָּרָשַׁת וָאֶתְחַנַּן.
עֲשֶׂרֶת הַדִּבְּרוֹת וּשְׁמַע יִשְׂרָאֵל בְּפָרָשַׁת וָאֶתְחַנַּן.
הַפָּרָשָׁה שֶׁלִּי מִסְפֵּר _____.

יוֹם-הַהֻלֶּדֶת שֶׁלִּי בַּ_____. בַּת הַמִּצְוָה שֶׁלִּי בְּחֹדֶשׁ חֶשְׁוָן.
אֲנִי _____ אֶת פָּרָשַׁת לֶךְ-לְךָ.
הַסִּפּוּר שֶׁל אַבְרָהָם וְשָׂרָה בְּפָרָשַׁת לֶךְ-לְךָ.
הַפָּרָשָׁה שֶׁלִּי מִסְפֵּר _____.

Here's how Mrs. Shapiro's students learned to read their Torah portions.

Because reading without vowels and punctuation can be tricky, a special book is used for learning to read a Torah portion. In this תִּקּוּן לַקּוֹרְאִים, the text of the whole Torah is printed twice. In one column, the text is presented in regular print with vowels. In the second column, it is printed in Torah script just as it appears in the Torah.

Practice reading the lines of the Priestly Blessing, Numbers 6: 24-26.
When you can read them in Torah script, go on to the next activity.

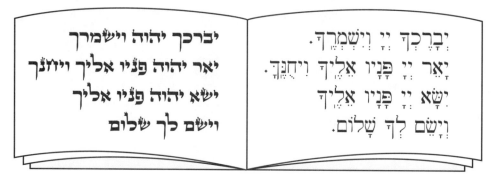

Imagine that it is your Bar or Bat Mitzvah. Recite the Torah blessings and read this passage from the Torah.

בָּרְכוּ אֶת־יְיָ הַמְבֹרָךְ. בָּרוּךְ יְיָ הַמְבֹרָךְ לְעוֹלָם וָעֶד.
בָּרוּךְ אַתָּה יְיָ אֱלֹהֵינוּ, מֶלֶךְ הָעוֹלָם, אֲשֶׁר בָּחַר בָּנוּ
מִכָּל־הָעַמִּים וְנָתַן לָנוּ אֶת־תּוֹרָתוֹ.
בָּרוּךְ אַתָּה יְיָ, נוֹתֵן הַתּוֹרָה.

בָּרוּךְ אַתָּה יְיָ אֱלֹהֵינוּ, מֶלֶךְ הָעוֹלָם, אֲשֶׁר נָתַן לָנוּ
תּוֹרַת אֱמֶת וְחַיֵּי עוֹלָם נָטַע בְּתוֹכֵנוּ.
בָּרוּךְ אַתָּה יְיָ, נוֹתֵן הַתּוֹרָה.

After the Torah has been read, a second biblical selection is read. This section is called the הַפְטָרָה (conclusion). The הַפְטָרָה is usually drawn from the writings of the Prophets, about whom you will learn in the next chapter.

"Our God Requires Truth and Justice."

דַף קְרִיאָה
READING PAGE

KEY WORD:
נְבִיאִים

Practice reading these words and phrases.

וְעַל-הַנְּבִיאִים	וּבִנְבִיאֵי	בַּנְּבִיאִים	נְבִיאִים	נָבִיא	.1
מִדְּבָרֶיךָ	דְּבָרָיו	וְנֶאֱמָנִים	נֶאֱמָן	וְרַחֲמָן	.2
אֶת-כְּבוֹדוֹ	שַׂמְּחֵנוּ	מְשַׂמֵּחַ	בְיָמֵינוּ	בִּמְהֵרָה	.3
בְּאֵלִיָּהוּ הַנָּבִיא	עַבְדֶּךָ	מְשִׁיחֶךָ	קָדְשֶׁךָ	דָּוִד	.4

.5 אֲשֶׁר בָּחַר בִּנְבִיאִים טוֹבִים

.6 שֶׁכָּל-דְּבָרָיו אֱמֶת וָצֶדֶק

.7 וּבִנְבִיאֵי הָאֱמֶת וָצֶדֶק

.8 יִתְבָּרַךְ שִׁמְךָ בְּפִי כָל-חַי

.9 צַדִּיק בְּכָל-הַדּוֹרוֹת, הָאֵל הַנֶּאֱמָן

.10 הָאוֹמֵר וְעוֹשֶׂה, הַמְדַבֵּר וּמְקַיֵּם

.11 וְרָצָה בְדִבְרֵיהֶם הַנֶּאֱמָרִים בֶּאֱמֶת

.12 אֲנַחְנוּ מוֹדִים לָךְ וּמְבָרְכִים אוֹתָךְ

.13 לִקְדֻשָּׁה וְלִמְנוּחָה, לְכָבוֹד וּלְתִפְאָרֶת

The נְבִיאִים (Prophets) called Israel to return to basic Jewish values.
In particular, they spoke of אֱמֶת and צֶדֶק — truth and justice.

Truth & Justice for Fun & Prophets

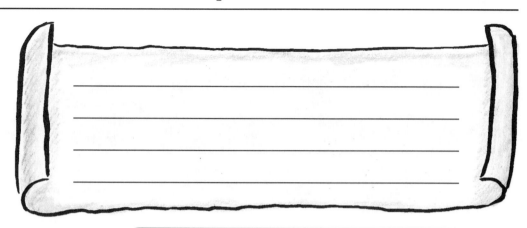

Read the quotes from each 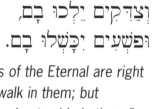 **נָבִיא** in Hebrew and English, then rewrite one of them as a message for people today.

כִּי-יְשָׁרִים דַּרְכֵי יְיָ
וְצַדִּקִים יֵלְכוּ בָם,
וּפֹשְׁעִים יִכָּשְׁלוּ בָם.

"For the ways of the Eternal are right and the just walk in them; but transgressors do stumble in them."
(Hosea 14:10)

וְשָׁכַן בַּמִּדְבָּר מִשְׁפָּט וּצְדָקָה בַּכַּרְמֶל תֵּשֵׁב.
וְהָיָה מַעֲשֵׂה הַצְּדָקָה שָׁלוֹם
וַעֲבֹדַת הַצְּדָקָה הַשְׁקֵט וָבֶטַח עַד-עוֹלָם.

"Then justice shall dwell in the wilderness and righteousness in the fruitful field. The effect of righteousness shall be peace and the work of righteousness shall be quietness and confidence forever." (Isaiah 32:16-17)

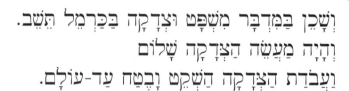

וְנִשְׁבַּעְתָּ חַי-יְיָ בֶּאֱמֶת בְּמִשְׁפָּט וּבִצְדָקָה,
וְהִתְבָּרְכוּ בוֹ גּוֹיִם וּבוֹ יִתְהַלָּלוּ.

"And you shall swear as the Eternal lives in truth, in justice and in righteousness; then shall the nations bless themselves by God and in God shall they glory." (Jeremiah 4:2)

וּמָה-יְיָ דּוֹרֵשׁ מִמְּךָ
כִּי אִם-עֲשׂוֹת מִשְׁפָּט וְאַהֲבַת חֶסֶד
וְהַצְנֵעַ לֶכֶת עִם-אֱלֹהֶיךָ.

"What does God require of you? Only to do justly, love mercy and walk humbly with your God." (Micah 6:8)

תּוֹרַת אֱמֶת הָיְתָה בְּפִיהוּ
וְעַוְלָה לֹא-נִמְצָא בִשְׂפָתָיו.

*"The Law of truth was in his mouth
and unrighteousness was not found
on his lips." (Malachi 2:6)*

בְּחֻקּוֹתַי יְהַלֵּךְ וּמִשְׁפָּטַי שָׁמַר לַעֲשׂוֹת אֱמֶת
צַדִּיק הוּא חָיֹה יִחְיֶה נְאֻם אֲדֹנָי יְהֹוִה.

*"One who walks in my laws and observes my statutes
to deal truthfully, this person is just and shall surely
live says the Eternal God." (Ezekiel 18:9)*

זֶה דְּבַר-יְיָ אֶל-זְרֻבָּבֶל לֵאמֹר: לֹא בְחַיִל
וְלֹא בְכֹחַ כִּי אִם-בְּרוּחִי אָמַר יְיָ צְבָאוֹת.

*"This is the word of the Eternal for Zerubabel:
Not by might nor by power, but by my spirit,
says Adonai of Hosts." (Zechariah 4:6)*

וְיִגַּל כַּמַּיִם מִשְׁפָּט
וּצְדָקָה כְּנַחַל אֵיתָן.

*"Let justice well up like waters
Righteousness as a mighty stream."
(Amos 5:24)*

1. How many times does a form of the word אֱמֶת appears in the quotes? _____

2. What does אֱמֶת mean? _____

3. The word צֶדֶק is derived from the Hebrew root .צ.ד.ק.
   How many words can you find that are derived from the root .צ.ד.ק? _____

4. What do words from the root .צ.ד.ק mean? _____ and justice

5. Multiply the number of times that a form of אֱמֶת appears by the number of times
   that a form of צֶדֶק appears (_____ X _____ = _____). This is the number of
   verses contained in most הַפְטָרָה readings.

Blessing Before Reading the Haftarah

Blessed are You Adonai our God,	בָּרוּךְ אַתָּה יְיָ אֱלֹהֵינוּ, .1
Sovereign of the universe,	מֶלֶךְ הָעוֹלָם, .2
Who has chosen good Prophets,	אֲשֶׁר בָּחַר בִּנְבִיאִים טוֹבִים, .3
desiring that they speak words of truth.	וְרָצָה בְדִבְרֵיהֶם הַנֶּאֱמָרִים בֶּאֱמֶת. .4
Blessed are You Adonai, Who chooses the Torah,	בָּרוּךְ אַתָּה יְיָ, הַבּוֹחֵר בַּתּוֹרָה, .5
and Moses Your servant and Israel Your people	וּבְמֹשֶׁה עַבְדּוֹ וּבְיִשְׂרָאֵל עַמּוֹ .6
and the Prophets of truth and justice.	וּבִנְבִיאֵי הָאֱמֶת וָצֶדֶק. .7

YIDBIT

While reading the Torah is biblically commanded, the custom of reading a section from the Prophets developed later. It was firmly in place before the second century C.E., when the Rabbis established the synagogue worship service. Many scholars believe that the reading of the הַפְטָרָה *can be traced to the Maccabean uprising in the second century B.C.E.*

When the Syrian king Antiochus became ruler of Judea, he banned most Jewish religious practices and prohibited public reading of the Torah on penalty of death. However, the Syrian rulers considered the writings of the נְבִיאִים *to be secular in nature. The Rabbis selected passages from the prophetic books that reflected the theme of each week's Torah portion. By publicly reading these passages, the teachings of the Torah were not forgotten.*

When the Maccabees defeated the Syrian forces, the regular public Torah reading was restored, but the custom of reading the הַפְטָרָה *was also retained.*

Supporting this theory is the odd fact that most הַפְטָרָה *readings contain the same number of verses. This number reminds us of the number of verses in a Torah reading. Each* עֲלִיָּה *to the Torah contains at least three verses, and traditionally there are seven* עֲלִיּוֹת *during the Shabbat service.*

How many verses do most הַפְטָרָה *readings contain?* _____
(Hint: Look back to pages 20 and 21.)

Haftarah Will Travel

The Haftarah portion for any Shabbat always contains one or more of the themes found in that week's Torah portion. Read the summaries of the Torah and Haftarah portions that follow. Find the Haftarah that best matches each Torah portion.

_____ וַיֵּרָא **(Gen. 18:1 - 22:24)**

The elderly Abraham and Sarah show great hospitality when three strangers appear at their tent. When the strangers announce the birth of a son, Sarah laughs. God destroys Sodom and Gomorrah. Sarah gives birth to Isaac. Hagar and Ishmael are sent away. God promises that Ishmael will found a great nation. God tests Abraham, demanding that he sacrifice Isaac, then saves Isaac at the last minute.

_____ וַיִּשְׁלַח **(Gen. 32:4 - 36:43)**

Returning home, Jacob passes through Esau's territory. Before meeting his brother, Jacob wrestles with an angel and prevails. He demands a blessing, and is given the name Israel. Jacob and Esau reconcile. Jacob settles in Shechem. His sons attack a local tribe after their sister is assaulted. Jacob travels to Bethel to build an altar. On the way, Rachel dies while giving birth to Benjamin. Isaac dies at the age of 180. Jacob and Esau bury their father.

_____ מִקֵּץ **(Gen. 41:1 - 44:17)**

Pharaoh, the King of Egypt, has dreams that no one can interpret. Pharaoh sends for Joseph, a Hebrew prisoner who interprets dreams. Joseph declares, "Egypt will have seven years of plenty followed by seven years of famine." Pharaoh puts Joseph in charge of food collection and storage. During the famine, Jacob sends his sons to Egypt to buy grain. Joseph recognizes his brothers, but they do not recognize him.

א **Hosea 11:7-12:12**

Hosea sends the message of God's undying love for Israel, even if Israel has strayed. Hosea depicts what Israel was meant to be, symbolized by incidents from the life of Jacob, and including a reference to Jacob's wrestling with an angel.

ב **First Kings 3:15-4:1**

Solomon, king of Israel, awakes from a dream in which he has asked God to grant him the gift of wisdom. Two women come to him. Both have recently given birth, but one child has died. Each claims to be the mother of the living baby. Solomon decrees: "Cut the baby in two and give each woman half." One woman agrees, but the other begs for the child's life. Solomon shows his wisdom by declaring that the second woman was the real mother because she cared for the child's life.

ג **Second Kings 4:1-37**

An older couple always showed great hospitality to Elisha (Elijah's disciple). Elisha predicts that they will have a son within a year, even though they are very old. When the son has grown up a bit, he goes out to the field to see his father. There he falls, hurts his head, and appears to die. Elisha saves the child.

The Twelve Gates

There are twelve gates through which the prayers of Israel ascend into heaven. Each tradition has its own gate. Thus, each Israelite should pray according to his or her own tradition so as not to bring confusion into the higher realms. (Rabbi Isaac Luria, 1534 - 1572)

Blessings after the Haftarah (Liberal Version)

Blessed are You Adonai our God,	בָּרוּךְ אַתָּה יְיָ אֱלֹהֵינוּ, 1.
Sovereign of the universe,	מֶלֶךְ הָעוֹלָם, 2.
Rock of all the world,	צוּר כָּל-הָעוֹלָמִים, 3.
The Just One in all generations, the faithful God,	צַדִּיק בְּכָל-הַדּוֹרוֹת, הָאֵל הַנֶּאֱמָן, 4.
Who speaks and does, Who decrees and fulfills,	הָאוֹמֵר וְעוֹשֶׂה, הַמְדַבֵּר וּמְקַיֵּם, 5.
Whose every word is truth and justice.	שֶׁכָּל-דְּבָרָיו אֱמֶת וָצֶדֶק. 6.
For the Torah and for the service,	עַל-הַתּוֹרָה וְעַל-הָעֲבוֹדָה 7.
and for the Prophets and for this Shabbat,	וְעַל-הַנְּבִיאִים וְעַל-יוֹם הַשַּׁבָּת הַזֶּה, 8.
which You have given us, Eternal our God,	שֶׁנָּתַתָּ-לָּנוּ, יְיָ אֱלֹהֵינוּ, 9.
for sanctity and rest, for honor and glory,	לִקְדֻשָּׁה וְלִמְנוּחָה, לְכָבוֹד וּלְתִפְאָרֶת, 10.
for all this, Eternal our God,	עַל-הַכֹּל, יְיָ אֱלֹהֵינוּ, 11.
we thank and bless You.	אֲנַחְנוּ מוֹדִים לָךְ וּמְבָרְכִים אוֹתָךְ. 12.
May Your Name be blessed by every living creature	יִתְבָּרַךְ שִׁמְךָ בְּפִי כָל-חַי 13.
always forever and ever.	תָּמִיד לְעוֹלָם וָעֶד. 14.
Blessed are You, Adonai, Who sanctifies Shabbat.	בָּרוּךְ אַתָּה יְיָ, מְקַדֵּשׁ הַשַּׁבָּת. 15.

☐ = added in Traditional Versions

Blessings after the Haftarah (Traditional Version)

Blessed are You Adonai our God,	בָּרוּךְ אַתָּה יְיָ אֱלֹהֵינוּ,	1.
Sovereign of the universe,	מֶלֶךְ הָעוֹלָם,	2.
Rock of all the world,	צוּר כָּל־הָעוֹלָמִים,	3.
The Just One in all generations, the faithful God,	צַדִּיק בְּכָל־הַדּוֹרוֹת, הָאֵל הַנֶּאֱמָן,	4.
Who speaks and does, Who decrees and fulfills,	הָאוֹמֵר וְעוֹשֶׂה, הַמְדַבֵּר וּמְקַיֵּם,	5.
Whose every word is truth and justice.	שֶׁכָּל־דְּבָרָיו אֱמֶת וָצֶדֶק.	6.

You are faithful Adonai our God	נֶאֱמָן אַתָּה הוּא יְיָ אֱלֹהֵינוּ	6א.
and faithful are Your words,	וְנֶאֱמָנִים דְּבָרֶיךָ,	6ב.
and not one of Your promises	וְדָבָר אֶחָד מִדְּבָרֶיךָ	6ג.
will remain unfulfilled,	אָחוֹר לֹא יָשׁוּב רֵיקָם,	6ד.
for You are a faithful and compassionate Sovereign.	כִּי אֵל מֶלֶךְ נֶאֱמָן וְרַחֲמָן אָתָּה.	6ה.
Blessed are You Eternal One,	בָּרוּךְ אַתָּה יְיָ,	6ו.
the God Who is faithful in all Your promises.	הָאֵל הַנֶּאֱמָן בְּכָל־דְּבָרָיו.	6ז.
Have compassion for Zion, the source of our life,	רַחֵם עַל צִיּוֹן כִּי הִיא בֵּית חַיֵּינוּ.	6ח.
and soon bring hope to the humble spirit,	וְלַעֲלוּבַת נֶפֶשׁ תּוֹשִׁיעַ בִּמְהֵרָה בְיָמֵינוּ.	6ט.
Blessed are You Adonai, Who brings joy to Zion.	בָּרוּךְ אַתָּה יְיָ, מְשַׂמֵּחַ צִיּוֹן בְּבָנֶיהָ.	6י.
Bring us joy through Elijah the Prophet,	שַׂמְּחֵנוּ יְיָ אֱלֹהֵינוּ בְּאֵלִיָּהוּ הַנָּבִיא עַבְדֶּךָ	6כ.
Your servant, and the Rule of David Your annointed.	וּבְמַלְכוּת בֵּית דָּוִד מְשִׁיחֶךָ.	6ל.
May Elijah come speedily to gladden our hearts,	בִּמְהֵרָה יָבֹא וְיָגֵל לִבֵּנוּ,	6מ.
May no outsider usurp David's throne	עַל כִּסְאוֹ לֹא יֵשֵׁב זָר	6נ.
and may no other inherit his glory,	וְלֹא יִנְחֲלוּ עוֹד אֲחֵרִים אֶת־כְּבוֹדוֹ,	6ס.
for by Your sacred Name You have promised	כִּי בְשֵׁם קָדְשְׁךָ נִשְׁבַּעְתָּ לּוֹ	6ע.
that his light will never be extinguished.	שֶׁלֹּא יִכְבֶּה נֵרוֹ לְעוֹלָם וָעֶד.	6פ.
Blessed are You Adonai, the Shield of David.	בָּרוּךְ אַתָּה יְיָ, מָגֵן דָּוִד.	6צ.

For the Torah and for the service	עַל הַתּוֹרָה וְעַל הָעֲבוֹדָה	7.
and for the Prophets and for this Shabbat,	וְעַל־הַנְּבִיאִים וְעַל יוֹם הַשַּׁבָּת הַזֶּה,	8.
which You have given us, Eternal our God,	שֶׁנָּתַתָּ־לָּנוּ, יְיָ אֱלֹהֵינוּ,	9.
for sanctity and rest, for honor and glory,	לִקְדֻשָּׁה וְלִמְנוּחָה, לְכָבוֹד וּלְתִפְאָרֶת,	10.
for all this, Eternal our God,	עַל הַכֹּל, יְיָ אֱלֹהֵינוּ,	11.
we thank and bless You.	אֲנַחְנוּ מוֹדִים לָךְ וּמְבָרְכִים אוֹתָךְ.	12.
May Your Name be blessed by every living creature	יִתְבָּרַךְ שִׁמְךָ בְּפִי כָּל־חַי	13.
always forever and ever.	תָּמִיד לְעוֹלָם וָעֶד.	14.
Blessed are You, Adonai, Who sanctifies Shabbat.	בָּרוּךְ אַתָּה יְיָ, מְקַדֵּשׁ הַשַּׁבָּת.	15.

אוֹצַר מִלִּים
A TREASURY OF WORDS

עוּגָה

עוּגוֹת

סֻכָּרִיָּה

סֻכָּרִיּוֹת

יְלָדִים גְּדוֹלִים   יְלָדִים קְטַנִּים   יְלָדוֹת גְּדוֹלוֹת   יְלָדוֹת קְטַנּוֹת

to buy = לִקְנוֹת	but = אֲבָל

Circle the phrase that matches each picture.

חַלּוֹת קְטַנּוֹת
חַלּוֹת גְּדוֹלוֹת
חַלָּה קְטַנָּה

דָּגִים קְטַנִּים
דָּגִים גְּדוֹלִים
דָּג גָּדוֹל

סֻכָּרִיָּה גְּדוֹלָה
סֻכָּרִיּוֹת טוֹבוֹת
עוּגוֹת יָפוֹת

עוּגוֹת טוֹבוֹת
עוּגוֹת קְטַנּוֹת
עוּגָה יָפָה

מְלוֹנִים יָפִים
בָּנָנוֹת יָפוֹת
בֵּיגְלִים יָפִים

חָלָב טוֹב
מְלוֹן יָפֶה
סֻכָּרִיָּה טוֹבָה

הוּא רוֹצֶה, הִיא רוֹצָה, סֻכָּרִיּוֹת בְּבַקָּשָׁה

In Ashkenazi synagogues, the Shabbat before the wedding is called a שַׁבַּת חָתָן or "Aufruf" in Yiddish. Sephardim have the שַׁבַּת חָתָן the first Shabbat after the wedding. Traditionally, the groom is given an עֲלִיָּה to the Torah, and is showered with candy. Today, in many Liberal congregations, both the bride and groom are honored with an עֲלִיָּה. After services, the couple's families often host a Kiddush.

Mrs. Shapiro's son is getting married next week. This week, she is making her purchases for the Kiddush, with some unexpected help.

בְּיוֹם שֵׁנִי בַּבֹּקֶר הַמּוֹרָה שָׁפִירוֹ הוֹלֶכֶת לַסּוּפֶּרְמַרְקֶט.
הִיא רוֹצָה לִקְנוֹת בֵּיגְלִים, דָּגִים, וְחָלָב.
יֵשׁ חָלָב וּבֵיגְלִים קְטַנִּים, אֲבָל אֵין דָּגִים.

בְּיוֹם שֵׁנִי בַּצָּהֳרַיִם שָׂרָה הוֹלֶכֶת לַסּוּפֶּרְמַרְקֶט.
הִיא רוֹצָה לִקְנוֹת סֻכָּרִיּוֹת טוֹבוֹת.

בְּיוֹם שְׁלִישִׁי בַּבֹּקֶר הַמּוֹרָה שָׁפִירוֹ הוֹלֶכֶת לִקְנוֹת דָּגִים.
כָּל הַדָּגִים יָפִים. הִיא רוֹאָה דָּגִים גְּדוֹלִים וּקְטַנִּים.
הִיא רוֹצָה דָּגִים קְטַנִּים.

בְּיוֹם שְׁלִישִׁי בָּעֶרֶב דָּנִי הוֹלֵךְ לַסּוּפֶּרְמַרְקֶט.
הוּא רוֹצֶה לִקְנוֹת סֻכָּרִיּוֹת קְטַנּוֹת.

בְּיוֹם רְבִיעִי בַּבֹּקֶר הַמּוֹרָה שָׁפִירוֹ רוֹצָה לִקְנוֹת עוּגוֹת.
הִיא רוֹצָה עוּגָה אַחַת גְּדוֹלָה וְיָפָה וְעוּגוֹת קְטַנּוֹת וְיָפוֹת.

בְּיוֹם חֲמִישִׁי בָּעֶרֶב רִבְקָה רוֹצָה לָלֶכֶת לַסוּפֶּרְמַרְקֶט.
רִבְקָה רוֹצָה לִקְנוֹת סֻכָּרִיּוֹת, אֲבָל אִמָּא שֶׁלָּה
רוֹפְאָה, וְהִיא לֹא אוֹהֶבֶת סֻכָּרִיּוֹת.
רִבְקָה לֹא הוֹלֶכֶת לַסוּפֶּרְמַרְקֶט.

בְּיוֹם שִׁשִּׁי בַּבֹּקֶר הַמּוֹרָה שָׁפִּירוֹ רוֹצָה שְׁתֵּי חַלּוֹת גְּדוֹלוֹת.

בְּיוֹם שִׁשִּׁי בַּצָּהֳרַיִם אֶסְתֵּר רוֹצָה לִקְנוֹת סֻכָּרִיּוֹת,
מִיכָאֵל רוֹצָה לִקְנוֹת סֻכָּרִיּוֹת,
וְגַם יוֹסִי רוֹצָה לִקְנוֹת סֻכָּרִיּוֹת.

בְּיוֹם שִׁשִּׁי בַּצָּהֳרַיִם הַמּוֹרָה שָׁפִּירוֹ הוֹלֶכֶת
לְבֵית הַכְּנֶסֶת עִם כָּל הָאֹכֶל.

In the calendar below, circle the items that were purchased each day.

יוֹם שִׁשִּׁי	יוֹם חֲמִישִׁי	יוֹם רְבִיעִי	יוֹם שְׁלִישִׁי	יוֹם שֵׁנִי
דָּגִים קְטַנִּים	בָּנָנוֹת יָפוֹת	עוּגוֹת קְטַנּוֹת	דָּגִים גְּדוֹלִים	חָלָב
סֻכָּרִיּוֹת	סֻכָּרִיּוֹת יָפוֹת	עוּגָה גְּדוֹלָה	חַלּוֹת גְּדוֹלוֹת	דָּגִים
חָלָב	מְלוֹנִים טוֹבִים	סֻכָּרִיּוֹת יָפוֹת	דָּגִים קְטַנִּים	בֵּיגְלִים קְטַנִּים
חַלּוֹת גְּדוֹלוֹת	דָּגִים גְּדוֹלִים	חַלּוֹת גְּדוֹלוֹת	סֻכָּרִיּוֹת קְטַנּוֹת	סֻכָּרִיּוֹת

The Torah, the Prophets and You

In the תּוֹרָה, Miriam, the sister of Moses and Aaron, is called מִרְיָם הַנְּבִיאָה. Miriam is one of the few women honored with this title. Both Moses and Miriam led the Children of Israel in song after they were wondrously saved at the Sea of Reeds. Here is part of what they sang. Study this passage with the vowels first, until you can read it easily without the vowels.

מִי-כָמֹכָה בָּאֵלִם יְיָ?

מִי כָּמֹכָה נֶאְדָּר בַּקֹּדֶשׁ?

נוֹרָא תְהִלֹּת עֹשֵׂה פֶלֶא.

מי כמכה באלם יהוה

מי כמכה נאדר בקדש

נורא תהלת עשה פלא

When this passage, called the Song of the Sea, is written in a Torah scroll a special pattern is used. Because this event was so important, the lines are written to represent the children of Israel walking between two walls of water. In most congregations, everyone stands when this song is read.

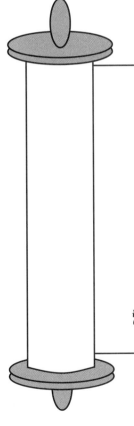

ברוזך כסמו ים   צללו כעופרת במים

אדירים   מי כמכה באלם יהוה   מי

כמכה נאדר בקדש   נורא תהלת עשה

פלא   נטית ימינך תבלעמן ארץ   נוזית

בוזסדך עם זו גאלת   נהלת בעזך אל מה

The Torah and Haftarah have both been read, so it is time to return the Torah to the Ark. You will learn about this in the next chapter.

CHAPTER 4

"The Torah Is Our Tree of Life."

סֵדֶר הַכְנָסַת הַתּוֹרָה

The Twelve Gates

KEY WORD:
עֵץ חַיִּים

There are twelve gates through which the prayers of Israel ascend into heaven. Each tradition has its own gate. Thus, each Israelite should pray according to his or her own tradition so as not to bring confusion into the higher realms.
(Rabbi Isaac Luria, 1534-1572)

Liberal Version

Let us praise the Name of the Eternal	יְהַלְלוּ אֶת־שֵׁם יְיָ 1.
for God's Name alone is exalted.	כִּי נִשְׂגָּב שְׁמוֹ לְבַדּוֹ. 2.
Your splendor covers heaven and earth,	הוֹדוֹ עַל אֶרֶץ וְשָׁמָיִם, 3.
You are the strength of Your people,	וַיָּרֶם קֶרֶן לְעַמּוֹ, 4.
making glorious Your faithful ones,	תְּהִלָּה לְכָל־חֲסִידָיו, 5.
the Children of Israel, a people close to You.	לִבְנֵי יִשְׂרָאֵל עַם קְרוֹבוֹ. 6.
Halleluyah!	הַלְלוּיָהּ! 7.
Behold, I have given you a good doctrine;	כִּי לֶקַח טוֹב נָתַתִּי לָכֶם, 8.
do not forsake it.	תּוֹרָתִי אַל־תַּעֲזֹבוּ. 9.
It is a tree of life to those who hold fast to it,	עֵץ־חַיִּים הִיא לַמַּחֲזִיקִים בָּהּ, 10.
and all who cling to it find happiness.	וְתֹמְכֶיהָ מְאֻשָּׁר. 11.
Its ways are ways of pleasantness,	דְּרָכֶיהָ דַרְכֵי־נֹעַם, 12.
and all its paths are peace.	וְכָל־נְתִיבוֹתֶיהָ שָׁלוֹם. 13.
Help us return to You, Adonai, then truly we shall return.	הֲשִׁיבֵנוּ יְיָ אֵלֶיךָ וְנָשׁוּבָה. 14.
Renew our days as of old.	חַדֵּשׁ יָמֵינוּ כְּקֶדֶם. 15.

Let us praise the Name of the Eternal,	1. יְהַלְלוּ אֶת־שֵׁם יְיָ
for God's Name alone is exalted.	2. כִּי נִשְׂגָּב שְׁמוֹ לְבַדּוֹ.
Your splendor covers heaven and earth,	3. הוֹדוֹ עַל אֶרֶץ וְשָׁמָיִם,
You are the strength of Your people,	4. וַיָּרֶם קֶרֶן לְעַמּוֹ,
making glorious Your faithful ones,	5. תְּהִלָּה לְכָל־חֲסִידָיו,
the Children of Israel, a people close to You.	6. לִבְנֵי יִשְׂרָאֵל עַם קְרוֹבוֹ.
Halleluyah!	7. הַלְלוּיָהּ!

NOTE: In Traditional congregations, Psalm 29 is recited here on Shabbat. See page 38.

And when the Ark was set down, Moses would say:	7א. וּבְנֻחֹה יֹאמַר:
Return, Adonai, to the myriad families of Israel.	7ב. שׁוּבָה יְיָ רִבְבוֹת אַלְפֵי יִשְׂרָאֵל.
Arise, Adonai, to Your sanctuary,	7ג. קוּמָה יְיָ לִמְנוּחָתֶךָ,
You and the Ark of Your strength.	7ד. אַתָּה וַאֲרוֹן עֻזֶּךָ.
May Your priests be clothed in justice,	7ה. כֹּהֲנֶיךָ יִלְבְּשׁוּ צֶדֶק,
and may Your faithful ones rejoice.	7ו. וַחֲסִידֶיךָ יְרַנֵּנוּ.
For the sake of David Your servant,	7ז. בַּעֲבוּר דָּוִד עַבְדֶּךָ,
Do not reject Your annointed.	7ח. אַל תָּשֵׁב פְּנֵי מְשִׁיחֶךָ.

Behold, I have given you a good doctrine;	8. כִּי לֶקַח טוֹב נָתַתִּי לָכֶם,
do not forsake it.	9. תּוֹרָתִי אַל־תַּעֲזֹבוּ.
It is a tree of life to those who hold fast to it,	10. עֵץ־חַיִּים הִיא לַמַּחֲזִיקִים בָּהּ,
and all who cling to it find happiness.	11. וְתֹמְכֶיהָ מְאֻשָּׁר.
Its ways are ways of pleasantness,	12. דְּרָכֶיהָ דַרְכֵי־נֹעַם,
and all its paths are peace.	13. וְכָל־נְתִיבוֹתֶיהָ שָׁלוֹם.
Help us return to You, Adonai, then truly we shall return.	14. הֲשִׁיבֵנוּ יְיָ אֵלֶיךָ וְנָשׁוּבָה.
Renew our days as of old.	15. חַדֵּשׁ יָמֵינוּ כְּקֶדֶם.

☐ = added in Traditional versions

In line 10 of this prayer, the Torah is described as an עֵץ־חַיִּים, a "tree of life."
Here are some other ways that the Torah is described.

Torah Is Like . . .

It has been said that the Torah has seventy faces. This allows different people to think of it in different ways. Read the Torah metaphors that follow, then create one of your own.

Its ways are ways of pleasantness and all its paths are peace. It is a tree of life for those who hold fast to it, and all who cling to it find happiness.

(Proverbs 3:17-18)

Light — this is Torah.

(Megillah 16b)

"The Torah is like a pomegranate. It is filled with words of wisdom as the pomegranate is full of seeds."

(Folk Proverb)

As waters reach from one end of the world to the other, so Torah reaches from one end of the world to the other. As water gives life to the world, so Torah gives life to the world. As waters are given without cost to the world, so Torah is given without cost to the world. As water is given from heaven, so Torah is given from heaven. As water is given to the accompaniment of powerful thundering, so was the Torah given with the accompaniment of powerful thundering. As water restores the human spirit, so Torah restores the human spirit.

(Song of Songs Rabbah 1:2)

"Words of Torah are like fine garments of Milesian wool. Just as garments of Milesian wool are difficult to acquire and are easily torn, so, too, words of Torah are difficult to acquire and are easily forgotten."

(Avot d'Rabbi Natan 31)

"Why are words of Torah compared to a fig tree? As with a fig tree, the more one tends it, the more figs one finds on it. So, too, with words of Torah: the more you study them, the more joy you find in them."

(Eruvin 54a-b)

Plenty of Plurals

Fill in the chart with the missing pronouns.

אַתֶּם

הִיא

אֲנִי

אַתָּה

הֵם

אֲנַחְנוּ

הֵן כּוֹתְבוֹת. הִיא כּוֹתֶבֶת. הֵם כּוֹתְבִים. הוּא כּוֹתֵב.

Study the verbs in the chart below.

having a great time = עוֹשִׂים חַיִּים
(masc. pl.)

one another = אֶחָד אֶת הַשֵּׁנִי

אוֹכְלוֹת	אוֹכְלִים	אוֹכֶלֶת	אוֹכֵל
נוֹתְנוֹת	נוֹתְנִים	נוֹתֶנֶת	נוֹתֵן
שׁוֹמְעוֹת	שׁוֹמְעִים	שׁוֹמַעַת	שׁוֹמֵעַ
רוֹאוֹת	רוֹאִים	רוֹאָה	רוֹאֶה
רוֹצוֹת	רוֹצִים	רוֹצָה	רוֹצֶה
עוֹשׂוֹת	עוֹשִׂים	עוֹשָׂה	עוֹשֶׂה

עֶרֶב שַׁבַּת חָתָן

Meanwhile, what are the bride and groom doing on Friday? Complete the story using verbs from the chart on page 34. Each item from the chart can be used only once. The first one has been done as an example.

יוֹם שִׁשִּׁי בַּבֹּקֶר, הֶחָתָן וְאַבָּא שֶׁלּוֹ
רוֹצִים לִקְנוֹת כִּפּוֹת לַחֲתֻנָה.
הֵם _____ כִּפּוֹת גְּדוֹלוֹת וְכִפּוֹת קְטַנּוֹת.

הַכַּלָּה וְאִמָּא שֶׁלָּה _____ לִקְנוֹת טַלִּית לֶחָתָן.
הֵן _____ טַלִּית גְּדוֹלָה וְיָפָה.

יוֹם שִׁשִּׁי בַּצָּהֳרַיִם, הֶחָתָן וְהַכַּלָּה בַּבַּיִת.
הֵם _____ אֶחָד אֶת הַשֵּׁנִי בַּטֶּלֶפוֹן.

יוֹם שִׁשִּׁי בָּעֶרֶב, הֶחָתָן, הַכַּלָּה,
וְכָל הַמִּשְׁפָּחָה _____ אֲרוּחַת עֶרֶב.
הַכַּלָּה _____ אֶת הַטַּלִּית לֶחָתָן.
הַמּוֹרָה שֶׁפָּרוֹ וְאִמָּא שֶׁל הַכַּלָּה
_____ חַלָּה וְסָלָט.

יוֹם שִׁשִּׁי בַּלַּיְלָה. לַיְלָה טוֹב
לְאַבָּא וְאִמָּא, לֶחָתָן וְגַם לַכַּלָּה.
אֲבָל הַיְלָדִים . . . _____ חַיִּים.

שַׁבַּת חָתָן

Write the number of the correct caption under each picture.

1. תָּמִי נוֹתֶנֶת סֻכָּרִיּוֹת טוֹבוֹת לַיְלָדִים.

2. הַחַזָּן קוֹרֵא אֶת הַפָּרָשָׁה בְּסֵפֶר הַתּוֹרָה.

3. הַתַּלְמִידוֹת בְּבֵית הַכְּנֶסֶת. הֵן מִתְפַּלְלוֹת.

4. בְּשַׁבָּת מִיכָאֵל וְיִצְחָק הוֹלְכִים לְבֵית הַכְּנֶסֶת.

5. בְּיוֹם שִׁשִּׁי בַּצׇּהֳרַיִם, הַיְלָדִים כּוֹתְבִים ״מַזָּל טוֹב״ לֶחָתָן וְלַכַּלָּה.

6. יֵשׁ סֻכָּרִיּוֹת עַל הַבִּימָה, בַּיָּדַיִם שֶׁל יוֹסִי, וּבַפֶּה שֶׁל יְהוֹשֻׁעַ.

7. יֵשׁ כּוֹסוֹת יַיִן בַּיָּדַיִם שֶׁל הַדּוֹד וְהַדּוֹדָה. הֵם שׁוֹמְעִים אֶת הַקִּדּוּשׁ.

8. לֹא רוֹאִים אֶת הֶחָתָן. הוּא תַּחַת הַטַּלִּית שֶׁלּוֹ.

9. אֵיפֹה רִבְקָה וְאֵיתָן? הֵם אוֹכְלִים סֻכָּרִיּוֹת וְעוּגוֹת. אִמָּא לֹא רוֹאָה.

_____

_____

_____

_____

_____

_____

_____

_____

_____

Prayerobics

In most Liberal congregations, the Torah is returned directly to the Ark after the Haftarah has been read. Traditional congregations read Psalm 29 on Shabbat and carry the Torah in a procession before it is returned to the Ark.

Psalm 29

A song of David.	מִזְמוֹר לְדָוִד.	.1
Acclaim to the Eternal all you mighty ones,	הָבוּ לַיְיָ בְּנֵי אֵלִים,	.2
Acclaim to the Eternal honor and strength.	הָבוּ לַיְיָ כָּבוֹד וָעֹז.	.3
Acclaim to the Eternal the honor of God's Name	הָבוּ לַיְיָ כְּבוֹד שְׁמוֹ	.4
Bow down to Adonai in the splendor of holiness.	הִשְׁתַּחֲווּ לַיְיָ בְּהַדְרַת קֹדֶשׁ.	.5
The voice of the Eternal calls above the waters,	קוֹל יְיָ עַל הַמָּיִם,	.6
the God of honor thunders,	אֵל הַכָּבוֹד הִרְעִים,	.7
the Eternal is above the great waters.	יְיָ עַל מַיִם רַבִּים.	.8
The voice of the Eternal echoes with strength,	קוֹל יְיָ בַּכֹּחַ,	.9
The voice of the Eternal echoes with majesty.	קוֹל יְיָ בֶּהָדָר.	.10
The voice of the Eternal shatters the cedars	קוֹל יְיָ שֹׁבֵר אֲרָזִים	.11
Adonai will shatter the cedars of Lebanon.	וַיְשַׁבֵּר יְיָ אֶת-אַרְזֵי הַלְּבָנוֹן.	.12
And they shall skip like calves,	וַיַּרְקִידֵם כְּמוֹ עֵגֶל,	.13
Lebanon and Syria like lambs.	לְבָנוֹן וְשִׂרְיוֹן כְּמוֹ בֶן-רְאֵמִים.	.14
The voice of Adonai ignites the lightning's fire,	קוֹל יְיָ חֹצֵב לַהֲבוֹת אֵשׁ,	.15
The voice of the Eternal shakes the wilderness,	קוֹל יְיָ יָחִיל מִדְבָּר,	.16
The Eternal will shake the wilderness of Kadesh.	יָחִיל יְיָ מִדְבַּר קָדֵשׁ.	.17
The voice of the Eternal makes the oaks tremble.	קוֹל יְיָ יְחוֹלֵל אַיָּלוֹת.	.18
God strips the forests bare,	וַיֶּחֱשֹׂף יְעָרוֹת,	.19
while in the sanctuary all declare God's glory.	וּבְהֵיכָלוֹ כֻּלּוֹ אֹמֵר כָּבוֹד.	.20
The Eternal sat enthroned during the flood,	יְיָ לַמַּבּוּל יָשָׁב,	.21
the Eternal shall be enthroned forever.	וַיֵּשֶׁב יְיָ מֶלֶךְ לְעוֹלָם.	.22
The Eternal will give strength to our people,	יְיָ עֹז לְעַמּוֹ יִתֵּן,	.23
The Eternal will bless our people with peace.	יְיָ יְבָרֵךְ אֶת-עַמּוֹ בַשָּׁלוֹם.	.24

According to the Talmud, when the Ten Commandments were given, the earth trembled and the air was filled with thunder and lightning. Psalm 29 describes this event, and gives us a clue about when it took place.

How many times does the phrase קוֹל יְיָ appear? _____

The Ten Commandments were given on the _____ day of the week,

which is also called _____.

For the Love of תּוֹרָה

The Torah is God's greatest gift. It symbolizes God's love for the Jewish people. The passage below contains the Torah's most elegant statement about the Jewish people's love for God. It is also written inside every מְזוּזָה. Study this passage, first with the vowels and then without them, until you can read it without the vowels.

וְאָהַבְתָּ אֵת יְהֹוָה אֱלֹהֶיךָ
בְּכָל־לְבָבְךָ וּבְכָל־נַפְשְׁךָ
וּבְכָל־מְאֹדֶךָ.
וְהָיוּ הַדְּבָרִים הָאֵלֶּה
אֲשֶׁר אָנֹכִי מְצַוְּךָ
הַיּוֹם עַל־לְבָבֶךָ.
וְשִׁנַּנְתָּם לְבָנֶיךָ וְדִבַּרְתָּ בָּם
בְּשִׁבְתְּךָ בְּבֵיתֶךָ
וּבְלֶכְתְּךָ בַדֶּרֶךְ
וּבְשָׁכְבְּךָ וּבְקוּמֶךָ.
וּקְשַׁרְתָּם לְאוֹת עַל־יָדֶךָ
וְהָיוּ לְטֹטָפֹת בֵּין עֵינֶיךָ.
וּכְתַבְתָּם עַל־מְזֻזוֹת בֵּיתֶךָ
וּבִשְׁעָרֶיךָ.

ואהבת את יהוה אלהיך
בכל לבבך ובכל נפשך
ובכל מאדך
והיו הדברים האלה
אשר אנכי מצוך
היום על לבבך
ושננתם לבניך ודברת בם
בשבתך בביתך
ובלכתך בדרך
ובשכבך ובקומך
וקשרתם לאות על ידך
והיו לטטפת בין עיניך
וכתבתם על מזוזת ביתך
ובשעריך

ואהבת את יהוה אלהיך בכל לבבך ובכל נפשך ובכל מאדך
והיו הדברים האלה אשר אנכי מצוך היום על לבבך
ושננתם לבניך ודברת בם בשבתך בביתך ובלכתך בדרך
ובשכבך ובקומך וקשרתם לאות על ידך והיו לטטפת בין
עיניך וכתבתם על מזוזת ביתך ובשעריך

Our devotion to Torah study and the worship of our unique God have always set the Jewish people apart and distinguished us for a special destiny. As the Jewish worship service concludes, it's time to explore our uniqueness.

CHAPTER 5

"We Praise God in Our Own Unique Way."

עָלֵינוּ

דַף קְרִיאָה
READING PAGE

KEY WORD:
אֲנַחְנוּ

Practice reading these words and phrases.

1. עָלֵינוּ   וַאֲנַחְנוּ   שָׂמָנוּ   עָשָׂנוּ   חֶלְקֵנוּ   וְגוֹרָלֵנוּ

2. לַאֲדוֹן   לְיוֹצֵר   לָתֵת   לְשַׁבֵּחַ   כְּגוֹיֵי   כְּכָל-הֲמוֹנָם

3. כּוֹרְעִים   וּמוֹדִים   מַלְכֵי   הַמְּלָכִים   וּמִשְׁתַּחֲוִים   כְּמִשְׁפָּחוֹת

4. שֶׁלֹּא עָשָׂנוּ כְּגוֹיֵי הָאֲרָצוֹת   5. וְלֹא שָׂמָנוּ כְּמִשְׁפְּחוֹת הָאֲדָמָה

6. שֶׁלֹּא שָׂם חֶלְקֵנוּ כָּהֶם   7. לִפְנֵי מֶלֶךְ מַלְכֵי הַמְּלָכִים

8. וַאֲנַחְנוּ כּוֹרְעִים וּמִשְׁתַּחֲוִים וּמוֹדִים

1. What suffix appears at the end of each word on line 1 above? _____

2. This suffix appears many times in the עָלֵינוּ prayer.
   Underline all the words ending with the suffix נוּ- in phrases 4 through 8.

3. Fill in the blanks to translate these words from the עָלֵינוּ.
   (Hint: the prayer appears on pages 42 and 43.)

and _____	= וַאֲנַחְנוּ	made us	= עָשָׂנוּ
_____ portion	= חֶלְקֵנוּ	_____	= אֲנַחְנוּ
_____ destiny	= גוֹרָלֵנוּ	_____ God	= אֱלֹהֵינוּ

4. The suffix נוּ- means _____ or _____.

This suffix appears frequently in our prayers. For a Jew, worship is more than an individual communication with God. Jewish prayer is often a communal offering. We use the suffix _____ when we talk to God about things that are common to all of _____.

Vive la Différence!

The עָלֵינוּ prayer talks about the idea that the Jewish people are different from other nations — not better, just different. How are we different? In ancient times, other nations bowed to idols, while our people worshiped one invisible God. Today, living in predominantly Christian countries where monotheism is virtually universal, it is sometimes hard to recognize how our religion requires different practices of us.

List three ways that the Jewish people are different today.

1. _____

2. _____

3. _____

For much of our history, Jews were forced to remain separate and distinct from the surrounding populations. We often had to live in separate neighborhoods and to wear distinctive clothing or yellow badges that identified us. We were not allowed to attend the same schools as others, and we were barred from many professions.

In today's society we are very similar to our neighbors in many ways. We are equal citizens with equal opportunities, and we share the same popular culture. Today, remaining different is actually a choice we must all make.

4. How does it make you feel to be different? (Check all with which you agree.)

    ❏ proud   ❏ scared

    ❏ embarrassed   ❏ strange

    ❏ honored   ❏ special

    ❏ nervous   ❏ happy

    ❏ content   ❏ other _____

5. Why should we choose to remain Jewish?

_____

_____

_____

When we recite the עָלֵינוּ, we are really saying, *"Vive la Différence!"*

The Twelve Gates

*Note: in some Liberal
congregations alternative versions
of the* עָלֵינוּ *are recited.*

It is our duty to worship the Ruler of everything	עָלֵינוּ לְשַׁבֵּחַ לַאֲדוֹן הַכֹּל	1.
to give praise to the Maker of Creation,	לָתֵת גְּדֻלָּה לְיוֹצֵר בְּרֵאשִׁית,	2.
Who did not make us like the nations of the lands,	שֶׁלֹּא עָשָׂנוּ כְּגוֹיֵי הָאֲרָצוֹת,	3.
and did not place us like the families of the earth,	וְלֹא שָׂמָנוּ כְּמִשְׁפְּחוֹת הָאֲדָמָה,	4.
Who did not make our portion like theirs,	שֶׁלֹּא שָׂם חֶלְקֵנוּ כָּהֶם,	5.
nor our destiny like all the others.	וְגוֹרָלֵנוּ כְּכָל-הֲמוֹנָם.	6.
And we bend our knees,	וַאֲנַחְנוּ כּוֹרְעִים	7.
and bow low, and give thanks	וּמִשְׁתַּחֲוִים וּמוֹדִים	8.
before the Ruler of all the Rulers	לִפְנֵי מֶלֶךְ מַלְכֵי הַמְּלָכִים	9.
The Holy and Blessed One.	הַקָּדוֹשׁ בָּרוּךְ הוּא.	10.
God stretched out the heavens	שֶׁהוּא נוֹטֶה שָׁמַיִם	11.
and established the earth,	וְיוֹסֵד אָרֶץ,	12.
Who dwells in the highest heavens above	וּמוֹשַׁב יְקָרוֹ בַּשָּׁמַיִם מִמַּעַל,	13.
and Whose strength rests in the heights.	וּשְׁכִינַת עֻזּוֹ בְּגָבְהֵי מְרוֹמִים.	14.
This is our God, there is none else.	הוּא אֱלֹהֵינוּ, אֵין עוֹד.	15.
In truth this is our incomparable Sovereign,	אֱמֶת מַלְכֵּנוּ, אֶפֶס זוּלָתוֹ,	16.
As it is written in the Torah:	כַּכָּתוּב בְּתוֹרָתוֹ:	17.
Know this day and take it to your heart,	וְיָדַעְתָּ הַיּוֹם וַהֲשֵׁבֹתָ אֶל-לְבָבֶךָ,	18.
that the Eternal is God in the heavens	כִּי יְיָ הוּא הָאֱלֹהִים בַּשָּׁמַיִם מִמַּעַל	19.
above and on the earth beneath,	וְעַל הָאָרֶץ מִתָּחַת,	20.
there is none else.	אֵין עוֹד.	21.

(In Traditional congregations, an additional paragraph is read silently here.)

And it has been said: The Eternal shall be acknowledged	וְנֶאֱמַר: וְהָיָה יְיָ	22.
as the Ruler of all the earth	לְמֶלֶךְ עַל כָּל-הָאָרֶץ:	23.
On that day, the Eternal shall be One	בַּיּוֹם הַהוּא יִהְיֶה יְהֹוָה אֶחָד	24.
and God's Name shall be One.	וּשְׁמוֹ אֶחָד.	25.

It is our duty to worship the Ruler of everything	עָלֵינוּ לְשַׁבֵּחַ לַאֲדוֹן הַכֹּל 1.
to give praise to the Maker of Creation,	לָתֵת גְּדֻלָּה לְיוֹצֵר בְּרֵאשִׁית, 2.
Who did not make us like the nations of the lands,	שֶׁלֹּא עָשָׂנוּ כְּגוֹיֵי הָאֲרָצוֹת, 3.
and did not place us like the families of the earth,	וְלֹא שָׂמָנוּ כְּמִשְׁפְּחוֹת הָאֲדָמָה, 4.
Who did not make our portion like theirs,	שֶׁלֹּא שָׂם חֶלְקֵנוּ כָּהֶם, 5.
nor our destiny like all the others,	וְגוֹרָלֵנוּ כְּכָל-הֲמוֹנָם, 6.
for they bow to vanity and emptiness	שֶׁהֵם מִשְׁתַּחֲוִים לְהֶבֶל וָרִיק א6.
and pray to a god that does not save.	וּמִתְפַּלְלִים אֶל אֵל לֹא יוֹשִׁיעַ. ב6.
And we bend our knees,	וַאֲנַחְנוּ כּוֹרְעִים 7.
and bow low, and give thanks	וּמִשְׁתַּחֲוִים וּמוֹדִים 8.
before the Ruler of all the Rulers	לִפְנֵי מֶלֶךְ מַלְכֵי הַמְּלָכִים 9.
The Holy and Blessed One.	הַקָּדוֹשׁ בָּרוּךְ הוּא. 10.
God stretched out the heavens	שֶׁהוּא נוֹטֶה שָׁמַיִם 11.
and established the earth,	וְיוֹסֵד אָרֶץ, 12.
Who dwells in the highest heavens above	וּמוֹשַׁב יְקָרוֹ בַּשָּׁמַיִם מִמַּעַל, 13.
and Whose strength rests in the heights.	וּשְׁכִינַת עֻזּוֹ בְּגָבְהֵי מְרוֹמִים. 14.
This is our God, there is none else.	הוּא אֱלֹהֵינוּ, אֵין עוֹד. 15.
In truth this is our incomparable Sovereign,	אֱמֶת מַלְכֵּנוּ, אֶפֶס זוּלָתוֹ, 16.
As it is written in the Torah:	כַּכָּתוּב בְּתוֹרָתוֹ: 17.
Know this day and take it to your heart,	וְיָדַעְתָּ הַיּוֹם וַהֲשֵׁבֹתָ אֶל-לְבָבֶךָ, 18.
that the Eternal is God in the heavens	כִּי יְיָ הוּא הָאֱלֹהִים בַּשָּׁמַיִם מִמַּעַל 19.
above and on the earth beneath,	וְעַל הָאָרֶץ מִתָּחַת, 20.
there is none else.	אֵין עוֹד. 21.

(An additional paragraph is read silently here.)

And it has been said: The Eternal shall be acknowledged	וְנֶאֱמַר: וְהָיָה יְיָ 22.
as the Ruler of all the earth	לְמֶלֶךְ עַל כָּל-הָאָרֶץ: 23.
On that day, the Eternal shall be One	בַּיּוֹם הַהוּא יִהְיֶה יְהֹוָה אֶחָד 24.
and God's Name shall be One.	וּשְׁמוֹ אֶחָד. 25.

☐ = added in Sephardic versions

Prayerobics

A special type of bowing is used during the עָלֵינוּ.

Originally, people bowed all the way to the ground, or "prostrated" themselves, when saying this line. That was the proper way to show respect for royalty in the ancient Near East. In some congregations it is customary to prostrate oneself when the Musaf עָלֵינוּ is recited during the High Holy Days.

Practice reading this line with the kind of bowing used in your congregation:

וַאֲנַחְנוּ כּוֹרְעִים וּמִשְׁתַּחֲוִים וּמוֹדִים לִפְנֵי מֶלֶךְ מַלְכֵי הַמְּלָכִים הַקָּדוֹשׁ בָּרוּךְ הוּא.

The עָלֵינוּ was originally recited only on רֹאשׁ הַשָּׁנָה as part of the service that crowns God Ruler of the Universe. Read on to find out how it became part of every service.

Yidbit

The עָלֵינוּ was added to the conclusion of each daily service after a terrible event that occurred during 1171 in Blois, France. The Jewish community of this tiny town was falsely accused of killing a Christian child and using his blood for ritual purposes. Thirty-three members of the community were burned at the stake when they refused to be baptized. As they died, they recited עָלֵינוּ as a reminder that we are different. The leading Rabbi of that day was Rashi's grandson, Rabbenu Tam. He wrote letters to every Jewish community informing them about what had taken place. Jewish communities worldwide added the עָלֵינוּ at the end of every service as a memorial to the martyrs.

Look back at pages 42 and 43. Notice that the Sephardim (Jews from Mediterranean lands and the Middle East) recite lines that are missing from the Ashkenazic version of the prayer. Write these lines out in Hebrew and in English.

Hebrew: _____

_____

וַאֲנַחְנוּ כּוֹרְעִים וּמִשְׁתַּחֲוִים וּמוֹדִים לִפְנֵי מֶלֶךְ מַלְכֵי הַמְּלָכִים הַקָּדוֹשׁ בָּרוּךְ הוּא.

English: _____

_____

And we bend our knees, and bow low, and give thanks before the Ruler of all the Rulers, The Holy and Blessed One.

The עָלֵינוּ was written in pagan times, when the most common style of worship was bowing before idols and making offerings of food, animals or even people to these statues. The lines above from the Sephardic עָלֵינוּ refer to idolatry, the worship of idols.

During the Middle Ages, Christian authorities censored the two lines that mention idol worship because they wrongly believed that these lines referred to Jesus in a negative manner. Surprisingly, in Moslem lands there was much less censorship of Jewish books. As a result, the Sephardic version of the עָלֵינוּ retained these lines.

Though our history is filled with painful events, our tradition emphasizes the importance of celebrating life. So we say, "May we only meet at happy events!"

אֵיפֹה אֲנַחְנוּ?

אוֹצֵר מִלִים
A TREASURY OF WORDS

of, belongs to =	שֶׁל
my, mine =	שֶׁלִי
your (masc. sing.) =	שֶׁלְךָ
your (fem. sing.) =	שֶׁלָךְ
his =	שֶׁלוֹ
hers =	שֶׁלָה
our =	שֶׁלָנוּ

Fill in the blanks with the correct form of the word שֶׁל*. You may use a form more than once.*

הַמִשְׁפָּחָה שֶׁל אִילָנָה בַּחֲתֻנָה.

הֵם בְּשֻׁלְחָן חָמֵשׁ.

אִילָנָה בֵּין הָאָחוֹת _____ וְהָאָח _____.

דָוִד הָאָח _____ אִילָנָה.

הוּא עַל-יַד אִילָנָה וְאִמָא _____.

מַזָּל טוֹב בַּחֲתֻנָּה לֶחָתָן וְלַכַּלָּה

Everyone's enjoying the wedding. Match the descriptions to the pictures.

_____ אֶסְתֵּר וְאִילָנָה   _____ בִּנְיָמִין וְיוֹסִי   הָאָב וְהָאֵם שֶׁל הֶחָתָן _____

1. הַיּוֹם הַחֲתֻנָּה שֶׁלָּנוּ. אֲנַחְנוּ אוֹהֲבִים אֶחָד אֶת הַשֵּׁנִי. אֲנַחְנוּ תַּחַת הַחֻפָּה.

2. אֲנַחְנוּ עוֹבְדִים בְּבֵית הַכְּנֶסֶת.

3. אֲנַחְנוּ אַחִים. הָאַבָּא שֶׁלָּנוּ רַבִּי.

4. הַמּוֹרָה שֶׁלָּנוּ אִמָּא שֶׁל הֶחָתָן. אֲנַחְנוּ שׁוֹמְעוֹת מוּסִיקָה טוֹבָה.

5. הַבַּת שֶׁלָּנוּ תַּלְמִידָה שֶׁל הַמּוֹרָה שַׁפִּירוֹ. אֲנַחְנוּ אוֹכְלִים אֲרוּחַת עֶרֶב.

6. אֲנַחְנוּ אַבָּא וְאִמָּא. הַבֵּן שֶׁלָּנוּ הֶחָתָן.

_____ הֶחָתָן וְהַכַּלָּה   הָאָב וְהָאֵם שֶׁל אִילָנָה _____   _____ הָרַבִּי וְהַחַזָּן

עָלֵינוּ לְשַׁבֵּחַ

On רֹאשׁ הַשָּׁנָה the עָלֵינוּ prayer is recited as part of the service that crowns God as Sovereign of the universe. Imagine that you are leading a coronation ceremony in which you proclaim God as the Sovereign of all space and all time. Now recite the עָלֵינוּ with your class.

עָלֵינוּ לְשַׁבֵּחַ לַאֲדוֹן הַכֹּל לָתֵת גְּדֻלָּה לְיוֹצֵר בְּרֵאשִׁית, שֶׁלֹּא עָשָׂנוּ כְּגוֹיֵי הָאֲרָצוֹת, וְלֹא שָׂמָנוּ כְּמִשְׁפְּחוֹת הָאֲדָמָה, שֶׁלֹּא שָׂם חֶלְקֵנוּ כָּהֶם, וְגוֹרָלֵנוּ כְּכָל-הֲמוֹנָם. וַאֲנַחְנוּ כּוֹרְעִים וּמִשְׁתַּחֲוִים וּמוֹדִים לִפְנֵי מֶלֶךְ מַלְכֵי הַמְּלָכִים הַקָּדוֹשׁ בָּרוּךְ הוּא.

The עָלֵינוּ prayer reminds us that we are part of a larger Jewish community which can give us tremendous comfort when times are bad. This support is especially meaningful when we lose someone important to us.

דַּף קְרִיאָה
READING PAGE

KEY WORD:
אָמֵן

1. וְאִמְרוּ: אָמֵן

2. דַּאֲמִירָן בְּעָלְמָא

3. וְיַמְלִיךְ מַלְכוּתֵהּ

4. תֻּשְׁבְּחָתָא וְנֶחֱמָתָא

5. בְּחַיֵּיכוֹן וּבְיוֹמֵיכוֹן

6. בַּעֲגָלָא וּבִזְמַן קָרִיב

7. יְהֵא שְׁמֵהּ רַבָּא מְבָרַךְ

8. וּבְחַיֵּי דְכָל־בֵּית יִשְׂרָאֵל

9. לְעָלַם וּלְעָלְמֵי עָלְמַיָּא

10. בְּעָלְמָא דִּי־בְרָא כִרְעוּתֵהּ

11. שְׁמֵהּ דְּקוּדְשָׁא, בְּרִיךְ הוּא

12. יִתְגַּדַּל וְיִתְקַדַּשׁ שְׁמֵהּ רַבָּא

13. יְהֵא שְׁלָמָא רַבָּא מִן־שְׁמַיָּא

14. וְחַיִּים עָלֵינוּ וְעַל־כָּל־יִשְׂרָאֵל

15. לְעֵלָּא מִן כָּל־בִּרְכָתָא וְשִׁירָתָא

16. וְיִתְנַשֵּׂא, וְיִתְהַדָּר וְיִתְעַלֶּה וְיִתְהַלָּל

17. יִתְבָּרַךְ וְיִשְׁתַּבַּח, וְיִתְפָּאַר וְיִתְרוֹמַם

The following phrase ends both the Mourner's קַדִּישׁ and the עֲמִידָה.
Practice reading it, then practice reading the entire קַדִּישׁ on page 50.

18. עֹשֶׂה שָׁלוֹם בִּמְרוֹמָיו הוּא יַעֲשֶׂה שָׁלוֹם עָלֵינוּ וְעַל כָּל־יִשְׂרָאֵל.

קַדִּישׁ יָתוֹם

The words of the קַדִּישׁ hold the power to bind heaven and earth.
The קַדִּישׁ can bring comfort during the time of our greatest pain,
affirming the goodness of life even in the face of loss and death.

Magnified and sanctified is God's great Name	1. יִתְגַּדַּל וְיִתְקַדַּשׁ שְׁמֵהּ רַבָּא
in this world which God created,	2. בְּעָלְמָא דִי בְרָא כִרְעוּתֵהּ,
may it be ruled under God's sovereignty	3. וְיַמְלִיךְ מַלְכוּתֵהּ
in our lives and our days	4. בְּחַיֵּיכוֹן וּבְיוֹמֵיכוֹן
and the life of the whole House of Israel,	5. וּבְחַיֵּי דְכָל־בֵּית יִשְׂרָאֵל,
soon and speedily,	6. בַּעֲגָלָא וּבִזְמַן קָרִיב,
and let us say: Amen.	7. וְאִמְרוּ: אָמֵן.
May God's great Name be blessed	8. יְהֵא שְׁמֵהּ רַבָּא מְבָרַךְ
now and forever.	9. לְעָלַם וּלְעָלְמֵי עָלְמַיָּא.
Blessed and praised, glorified	10. יִתְבָּרַךְ וְיִשְׁתַּבַּח, וְיִתְפָּאַר וְיִתְרוֹמַם
and exalted, adorned, and lauded	11. וְיִתְנַשֵּׂא, וְיִתְהַדָּר וְיִתְעַלֶּה וְיִתְהַלָּל
is the Name of the Holy and Blessed One,	12. שְׁמֵהּ דְּקוּדְשָׁא, בְּרִיךְ הוּא,
above all blessing and song,	13. לְעֵלָּא מִן כָּל־בִּרְכָתָא וְשִׁירָתָא,
psalm, or praise that can be uttered	14. תֻּשְׁבְּחָתָא וְנֶחֱמָתָא
in this world, and let us say: Amen.	15. דַּאֲמִירָן בְּעָלְמָא, וְאִמְרוּ: אָמֵן.
Let there be abundant peace from heaven,	16. יְהֵא שְׁלָמָא רַבָּא מִן שְׁמַיָּא,
and life for us and for all Israel,	17. וְחַיִּים עָלֵינוּ וְעַל־כָּל־יִשְׂרָאֵל,
and let us say: Amen.	18. וְאִמְרוּ: אָמֵן.
May the One Who makes peace in the heavens,	19. עֹשֶׂה שָׁלוֹם בִּמְרוֹמָיו,
make peace for us	20. הוּא יַעֲשֶׂה שָׁלוֹם עָלֵינוּ
and for all Israel,	21. וְעַל כָּל־יִשְׂרָאֵל,
and let us say: Amen.	22. וְאִמְרוּ אָמֵן.

The קַדִּישׁ and עֲמִידָה end with the same phrase, accompanied by special actions.

Prayerobics

In some congregations, only those mourning their parents, siblings, spouses, or children rise to say the קַדִּישׁ. The act of saying this prayer is thus kept sacred for mourning the loss of one's closest relatives. In other congregations, all worshipers rise to say the קַדִּישׁ. In this way, the entire community lends its support to those who mourn. At the same time, it gives worshipers the opportunity to say קַדִּישׁ for the six million Jews martyred in the Holocaust, many of whom have no one to say קַדִּישׁ for them.

When we reach the end of the קַדִּישׁ, we are leaving God's presence, just as we leave God's "royal court" at the conclusion of the עֲמִידָה. A set of special actions is used when we leave God's presence. Here's how it works.

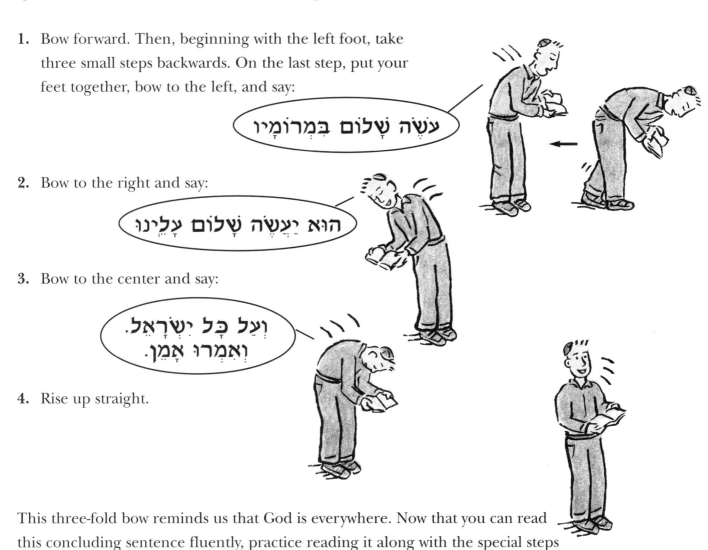

1. Bow forward. Then, beginning with the left foot, take three small steps backwards. On the last step, put your feet together, bow to the left, and say:

   עֹשֶׂה שָׁלוֹם בִּמְרוֹמָיו

2. Bow to the right and say:

   הוּא יַעֲשֶׂה שָׁלוֹם עָלֵינוּ

3. Bow to the center and say:

   וְעַל כָּל יִשְׂרָאֵל. וְאִמְרוּ אָמֵן.

4. Rise up straight.

This three-fold bow reminds us that God is everywhere. Now that you can read this concluding sentence fluently, practice reading it along with the special steps that accompany it until you can coordinate your words and actions.

עֹשֶׂה שָׁלוֹם בִּמְרוֹמָיו, הוּא יַעֲשֶׂה שָׁלוֹם עָלֵינוּ וְעַל כָּל-יִשְׂרָאֵל, וְאִמְרוּ אָמֵן.

The Mysterious Origins of the קַדִּישׁ

The קַדִּישׁ was not originally part of the synagogue service.
Rather, it was recited by teachers at the end of a study session.
The Talmud records that the students would respond by saying:

אָמֵן. יְהֵא שְׁמֵהּ רַבָּא מְבָרַךְ לְעָלַם וּלְעָלְמֵי עָלְמַיָּא.

When the קַדִּישׁ became a part of the synagogue service, it was recited after the Torah reading, signaling the end of the Torah service. Gradually, different forms of the קַדִּישׁ were used to end the various parts of the service. To this day, the קַדִּישׁ is still used to separate parts of the service.

How did the קַדִּישׁ come to be associated with mourning? Long ago, it was customary to hold a study session during *Shivah*, the seven-day period of intense mourning. This session honored a deceased member of the community. At the end of this session, the קַדִּישׁ was recited. Gradually, the study session grew less common, but reciting the קַדִּישׁ grew in importance, until it became the central part of the mourning ritual.

COUSIN LANGUAGES

Aramaic is a language that is closely related to Hebrew. The Aramaic phrase קֻדְשָׁא בְּרִיךְ הוּא *is the same as the Hebrew phrase* הַקָּדוֹשׁ בָּרוּךְ הוּא *("the Holy and Blessed One"). Read the Hebrew and Aramaic words out loud, then write your translations of them.*

English	Aramaic	Hebrew
_____	לָא	לֹא
_____	עָלַם	עוֹלָם
_____	אַרְעָא	אֶרֶץ
_____	שְׁלָמָא	שָׁלוֹם
_____	טֵב	טוֹב
_____	חַד	אֶחָד
_____	אַבָּא	אָב
_____	אִמָּא	אֵם
_____	לַחְמָא	לֶחֶם
_____	כַּלְבָּא	כֶּלֶב
_____	מַיָּא	מַיִם
_____	אֱלָהִין	אֱלֹהִים

When we say קַדִּישׁ, we are preserving the memory of someone very important to us.
The word קַדִּישׁ itself is related to a very special Hebrew word family.

קָדוֹשׁ, קָדוֹשׁ, קָדוֹשׁ

Fill in each blank with the correct word from the word box.

WORD BOX
יַיִן
אֵין
קָדוֹשׁ
תּוֹרָה
חָתָן
קוֹרֵאת

1. אַבָּא עוֹשֶׂה קִדוּשׁ עִם _____ טוֹב.

2. בְּבֵית הַכְּנֶסֶת יֵשׁ סֵפֶר _____ בַּאֲרוֹן הַקֹּדֶשׁ.

3. _____ בֵּית מִקְדָּשׁ הַיּוֹם בִּירוּשָׁלַיִם.

4. בַּחֲתֻנָּה יֵשׁ קִדּוּשִׁין בֵּין _____ וְכַלָּה.

5. אֶסְתֵּר _____ אֶת פָּרָשַׁת ״קְדוֹשִׁים״ בְּבַת הַמִּצְוָה שֶׁלָּהּ.

6. בַּעֲמִידָה הַחַזָּן מִתְפַּלֵּל: ״קָדוֹשׁ _____ קָדוֹשׁ.״

Each of the sentences above contains a form of the root word .קָ.ד.שׁ.
Circle these words. Members of this word family are often translated as
"holy," but are better defined as "sacred," "special," or "set apart."

Fill in the correct form of the root word .קָ.ד.שׁ to match the pictures below.
Use the sentences above to help you.

_____   _____   _____   _____

How are each of these things "special" or "set apart"? _____

_____

Root Word Crossword

Use the word box to fill in the missing word in each sentence below.
Then transfer those words to the crossword puzzle.

ACROSS

‎3. הַיְלָדִים _ _ _ _ _ אֶת כָּל הַפָּרָשָׁה.

‎5. אֶסְתֵּר _ _ _ _ _ אֶת פָּרָשַׁת קְדוֹשִׁים עִם הַחַזָּן.

‎6. יֵשׁ _ _ _ עֲלִיּוֹת לַתּוֹרָה בְּשַׁבָּת.

‎8. לְדָנִי יֵשׁ בַּר-מִצְוָה בְּחֹדֶשׁ אִיָּר.

גַּם לְאֶסְתֵּר יֵשׁ בַּת-מִצְוָה בְּחֹדֶשׁ אִיָּר.

_ _ לוֹמְדִים לִקְרֹא בַּתּוֹרָה.

DOWN

‎1. אֶסְתֵּר כּוֹתֶבֶת אֶת דְּבַר הַתּוֹרָה שֶׁלָּהּ, וְדָנִי _ _ _ _ אֶת דְּבַר הַתּוֹרָה שֶׁלּוֹ.

‎2. דָּנִי: "בַּר הַמִּצְוָה שֶׁלִּי וּבַת הַמִּצְוָה שֶׁלָּהּ בְּשַׁבָּת אַחַת."

הַפָּרָשָׁה _ _ _ _ קְדוֹשִׁים.

‎4. דָּנִי וְאֶסְתֵּר _ _ _ _ גְּדוֹלִים.

‎7. גַּם דָּנִי לוֹמֵד אֶת פָּרָשַׁת קְדוֹשִׁים _ _ הַחַזָּן.

WORD BOX

הֵם

עִם

שֶׁבַע

שֶׁלָּנוּ

כּוֹתֵב

יְלָדִים

לוֹמֶדֶת

קוֹרְאִים

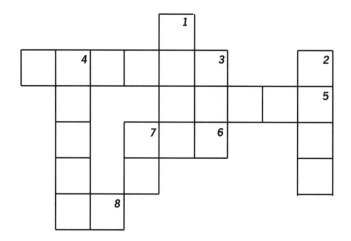

The three root letters in the shaded box (3 down) mean _____

The name of this chapter's prayer is derived from these three root letters.

When You Really Count

KEY WORD:
אָמֵן

When mourners recite קַדִּישׁ, they need someone to say "אָמֵן". For this reason, the קַדִּישׁ is traditionally recited only when a מִנְיָן is present. A מִנְיָן (literally "counting") is a community of at least ten adult Jews. In Orthodox congregations, only men are counted in a מִנְיָן. In Reform, Conservative, and Reconstructionist congregations, both men and women are counted. When you become Bar or Bat Mitzvah, you are considered to be a Jewish adult who can say "אָמֵן" as part of the community. Practice reading the קַדִּישׁ.

יִתְגַּדַּל וְיִתְקַדַּשׁ שְׁמֵהּ רַבָּא בְּעָלְמָא דִּי בְרָא כִרְעוּתֵהּ,
וְיַמְלִיךְ מַלְכוּתֵהּ בְּחַיֵּיכוֹן וּבְיוֹמֵיכוֹן וּבְחַיֵּי דְכָל־בֵּית יִשְׂרָאֵל,
בַּעֲגָלָא וּבִזְמַן קָרִיב, וְאִמְרוּ: אָמֵן.
יְהֵא שְׁמֵהּ רַבָּא מְבָרַךְ לְעָלַם וּלְעָלְמֵי עָלְמַיָּא.
יִתְבָּרַךְ וְיִשְׁתַּבַּח, וְיִתְפָּאַר וְיִתְרוֹמַם וְיִתְנַשֵּׂא, וְיִתְהַדָּר
וְיִתְעַלֶּה וְיִתְהַלָּל שְׁמֵהּ דְּקֻדְשָׁא, בְּרִיךְ הוּא,
לְעֵלָּא מִן כָּל־בִּרְכָתָא וְשִׁירָתָא, תֻּשְׁבְּחָתָא וְנֶחֱמָתָא
דַּאֲמִירָן בְּעָלְמָא, וְאִמְרוּ: אָמֵן.
יְהֵא שְׁלָמָא רַבָּא מִן שְׁמַיָּא וְחַיִּים עָלֵינוּ וְעַל כָּל־יִשְׂרָאֵל, וְאִמְרוּ: אָמֵן.
עֹשֶׂה שָׁלוֹם בִּמְרוֹמָיו, הוּא יַעֲשֶׂה שָׁלוֹם עָלֵינוּ
וְעַל כָּל־יִשְׂרָאֵל, וְאִמְרוּ: אָמֵן.

Way back at the beginning of Book 2, you learned about the אֵין כֵּאלֹהֵינוּ prayer. אֵין כֵּאלֹהֵינוּ is an acrostic poem. The first letter of each verse is in the column on the right.

Rashi teaches that saying the end of any blessing (אָמֵן) followed by the opening phrase (בָּרוּךְ אַתָּה) reminds us that our praises for God should never end. Thus, even though the service concludes following קַדִּישׁ יָתוֹם, Jewish prayer is a never ending cycle.

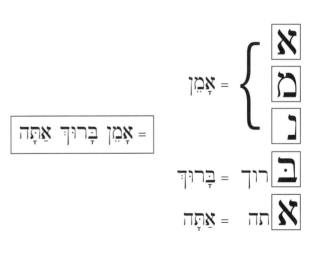

אָמֵן = {
אָמֵן בָּרוּךְ אַתָּה =
בָּרוּךְ = רוּך
אַתָּה = תה

CHAPTER 7

"Prayer To Our God Never Ends."

זְמַן לִתְפִילָה

Complete the charts with the names of the prayers. Answer the questions on page 58.

KEY WORD:
בָּרוּךְ אַתָּה

The מַעֲרִיב/ עַרְבִית Service
Opening Prayers, Blessings, Psalms or Passages of Praise
The שְׁמַע and Its Blessings   Call to Worship: בָּרְכוּ   Creation: _____   Torah: _____   שְׁמַע   וְאָהַבְתָּ   God Saves Israel: _____ & _____   Protect Us at Night: הַשְׁכִּיבֵנוּ
עֲמִידָה   אָבוֹת   גְבוּרוֹת   קְדֻשַׁת הַשֵׁם   קְדֻשַׁת הַיוֹם *or Weekday Petitions*   עֲבוֹדָה   הוֹדָאָה   שָׁלוֹם רָב
Torah Service   *(May be added here on Shabbat & Festivals in Liberal settings)*
Concluding Prayers   עָלֵינוּ   קַדִּישׁ יָתוֹם   **Closing Prayer or Psalm**

There are three Jewish daily worship services: שַׁחֲרִית, the morning service; מִנְחָה, the afternoon service; and the evening service, which Ashkenazic Jews call מַעֲרִיב and Sephardic Jews call עַרְבִית. In traditional congregations, there is an additional service right after the morning service on Shabbat. It is called מוּסָף.

The three daily services all begin with opening prayers, blessings, Psalms, or passages of praise. These vary greatly from service to service.

The מַעֲרִיב/עַרְבִית and שַׁחֲרִית services begin with the בָּרְכוּ, and include the שְׁמַע and its Blessings. This section focuses on the themes of creation (the מַעֲרִיב עֲרָבִים in the evening and the יוֹצֵר אוֹר in the morning); Torah (אַהֲבַת עוֹלָם in the evening and אַהֲבָה רַבָּה in the morning); and the idea that God rescues Israel (מִי-כָמֹכָה and אֱמֶת).

The עֲמִידָה is the core of every Jewish worship service, although the text for each service contains some variations.

The three daily services (מִנְחָה, שַׁחֲרִית, and מַעֲרִיב/עַרְבִית) all end with קַדִּישׁ, עָלֵינוּ, and a closing prayer, such as אֲדוֹן עוֹלָם.

עֶרֶב וָבֹקֶר וְצָהֳרִים

The מִנְחָה Service	The שַׁחֲרִית Service
Opening Psalm (אַשְׁרֵי)	Opening Prayers, Blessings, Psalms or Passages of Praise
עֲמִידָה ――――――― ――――――― קְדֻשָׁה קְדֻשַּׁת הַיּוֹם or Weekday Petitions עֲבוֹדָה הוֹדָאָה שָׁלוֹם רָב	**The שְׁמַע and Its Blessings** Call to Worship: בָּרְכוּ Creation: ――――――― Torah: ――――――― שְׁמַע וְאָהַבְתָּ God Saves Israel: ――――――― & ―――――――
Additional Prayers (including Psalm of the Day)	עֲמִידָה ――――――― ――――――― קְדֻשָׁה קְדֻשַּׁת הַיּוֹם or Weekday Petitions ――――――― ――――――― שִׂים שָׁלוֹם
Torah Service (Shabbat & Festivals Only)	
Concluding Prayers עָלֵינוּ קַדִּישׁ יָתוֹם Closing Prayer or Psalm	**Torah Service** (Shabbat, Festivals, New Jewish Months, Mondays & Thursdays Only)
The מוּסָף Service	**Concluding Prayers** עָלֵינוּ קַדִּישׁ יָתוֹם Closing Prayer or Psalm
(Shabbat & Festival Mornings Only, Before Concluding Prayers) עֲמִידָה	
אֵין כֵּאלֹהֵינוּ	

עֲבוֹדָה שֶׁהִיא בַּלֵּב
A Service of the Heart

1. In the עַרְבִית/מַעֲרִיב service, a fourth blessing can be found in the section known as "The שְׁמַע and Its Blessings". It asks God to protect us at night. What is it called?

   _____

2. The first two blessings of the עֲמִידָה are always the same. The first describes the relationship our ancestors had with God. What is it called?

   _____

   The second blessing describes God's heroic powers. What is it called?

   _____

3. The third blessing of the עֲמִידָה always reminds us that God is set apart, or is unlike anything else in the universe. In Hebrew, the word קָדוֹשׁ describes this uniqueness. What blessing is recited during the שַׁחֲרִית and מִנְחָה services?

   _____

   What blessing is recited during the עַרְבִית/מַעֲרִיב service or whenever the עֲמִידָה is recited silently?

   _____

4. On weekdays, a series of petitions are recited between the first three and last three blessings of the עֲמִידָה. What blessing replaces these petitions on Shabbat and Festivals?

   _____

5. Three blessings are found at the end of the עֲמִידָה. Which two of these blessings are always the same?

   _____

   _____

6. At the end of every עֲמִידָה we find a blessing for peace. There are two different versions. Which blessing is recited in the עַרְבִית/מַעֲרִיב and מִנְחָה service?

   _____

   Which is recited during the שַׁחֲרִית service?

   _____

7. When is a Torah service included in your congregation?

   _____

8. The three daily services (מִנְחָה, שַׁחֲרִית, and עַרְבִית/מַעֲרִיב) all end with a closing prayer, such as אָדוֹן עוֹלָם. Two other prayers always precede the closing prayer or Psalm. What are they?

   _____

   _____

   Now that you understand the structure of the Jewish worship service, take a look at Danny and Esther's B'nai Mitzvah service.

בַּר הַמִצְוָה שֶׁלוֹ... בַּת הַמִצְוָה שֶׁלָה...

Read the sentences that follow. Check the box to indicate whether an event
or item can be found in Picture א, in Picture ב, or not at all.

Picture ב

Picture א

Not Pictured	Picture ב	Picture א	
☐	☐	☐	1. אֶסְתֵּר עוֹמֶדֶת עַל הַבִּימָה.
☐	☐	☐	2. הָרַבִּי נוֹתֵן אֶת סֵפֶר הַתּוֹרָה לְדָנִי.
☐	☐	☐	3. דָּנִי מִתְפַּלֵּל "שְׁמַע יִשְׂרָאֵל" עִם הַיָּד שֶׁלוֹ עַל הָעֵינַיִם שֶׁלוֹ.
☐	☐	☐	4. דָּנִי בְּבֵית-חוֹלִים. הוּא חוֹלֶה.
☐	☐	☐	5. יֵשׁ לְדָנִי טַלִּית יָפָה עַל הָרֹאשׁ.
☐	☐	☐	6. אֶסְתֵּר עוֹמֶדֶת בֵּין אַבָּא וְאִמָּא שֶׁלָה.
☐	☐	☐	7. הַיּוֹם בַּבֹּקֶר אִמָּא שֶׁל אֶסְתֵּר עוֹבֶדֶת בַּסִּפְרִיָּה.
☐	☐	☐	8. הַתַּלְמִידִים רוֹאִים אֶת דָּנִי בְּבַר הַמִצְוָה שֶׁלוֹ.
☐	☐	☐	9. אֵיפֹה דָּנִי וְאֶסְתֵּר הַיּוֹם? הֵם הוֹלְכִים לְרוֹפֵא.
☐	☐	☐	10. אִמָּא וְאַבָּא שֶׁל אֶסְתֵּר כּוֹתְבִים מִכְתָּבִים.
☐	☐	☐	11. שָׂרָה שׁוֹמַעַת אֶת הַתְּפִלָּה.
☐	☐	☐	12. יֵשׁ כּוֹכָבִים יָפִים בַּלַּיְלָה.
☐	☐	☐	13. אֶסְתֵּר קוֹרֵאת בְּעִבְרִית מִסֵּפֶר הַתּוֹרָה.

Danny and Esther led the congregation in prayer and read from the Torah.

Take a look now at the last words on these subjects.

CHAPTER **7**

The First Word and the Final Word

Unscramble the Key Words and prayer names below.

1. They taught אֱמֶת and צֶדֶק to Israel ___ ◯ ___ ___ ◯ ___ = אִינְבִים

2. A Torah scroll's house ◯ ___ ___ ___ ___ ◯ ___ = רוֹאֶן דֶּהַקֹּשׁ

3. The final word of many prayers ___ ___ ◯ = מָאֵן

4. 54 Portions, 79,976 Words, 304,805 Letters ___ ___ ___ ◯ = רְתּוֹה

5. The first words of a blessing ___ ___ ___ ___ ◯ ___ = רוּבְךָ תָּאַה

6. Prayer of memory and honor ___ ___ ___ ◯ ◯ ___ ___ ___ = דִּיקַשׁ תוֹיָם

7. We ___ ___ ___ ___ ◯ = נַחְאָנוּ

8. Prayer that says we are different ___ ___ ___ ◯ ___ = נוּעָלֵי

List the letters that are circled above. Do not add vowels or other markings.
Unscramble the letters to find the first and last words in the Torah.

The first word in the Torah: ___ ___ ___ ___ ___ ___
(Hint: It is also the name of the first book in the Torah.)

The last word in the Torah: ___ ___ ___ ___ ___ (Hint: It is also the name of our first homeland.)

In his very first comment on the Torah, Rashi quotes Rabbi Isaac (most likely Rashi's own father). Rabbi Isaac taught that since the Torah is a book of מִצְוֹת for the people of Israel, it should really begin with the verse "This month you shall mark for yourselves the beginning of all months" (Exodus 12:2), as this is the first major מִצְוָה given to the Children of Israel. Rashi states that the Torah begins with the creation of the universe to show that God, as Creator, had the right to give the land of Israel to the people of Israel.

Another way of looking at the connection between the end of the Torah and its beginning is to connect the last letter of the Torah with the first letter of the Torah, just as we do with our readings on Simchat Torah.

First letter in the Torah ⟶ _____ _____ ⟵ *Last letter in the Torah*

1. What does this Hebrew word mean? _____
2. What does this tell you about the Torah? _____

Rashi was one of the greatest Torah teachers of all time.
At your Bar or Bat Mitzvah, you may also teach about the Torah.

CHAPTER 7   60

דְּבַר תּוֹרָה

Danny stepped up to the podium. He looked out at the congregation and smiled. "Today I am a man," he began. After his friends stopped laughing, Danny explained. "Okay — so I may not be able to drive a car or vote yet. My Dad isn't going to send me out to fend for myself, even though he might want to! Becoming a Bar Mitzvah means that I now have all the rights and responsibilities as an adult in the Jewish community.

"In preparing for this day, we have learned a lot. We studied Hebrew, and learned to speak a little of our own holy language. To my Israeli family, I would just like to say: תּוֹדָה רַבָּה, both for treating me to such a wonderful visit last year, and for coming all the way from אֶרֶץ יִשְׂרָאֵל to be with me today."

Esther spoke next. "Danny said תּוֹדָה רַבָּה, which is how we say thank you in Hebrew. We both want to thank our entire families, for their love and support, especially our parents. Mom, Dad, תּוֹדָה רַבָּה.

"We also want to thank our teacher, Mrs. Shapiro," Esther continued. "She not only taught us how to read our prayers, she taught us what they really mean. From Mrs. Shapiro, we learned that Jewish prayer helps us to remember what is really important and what we should be doing to make the world a better place."

"That's the lesson of this week's Torah portion, פָּרָשַׁת קְדוֹשִׁים," Danny added. "The Hebrew word קְדוֹשִׁים can be translated as 'holy,' 'set apart,' or 'special.' And פָּרָשַׁת קְדוֹשִׁים gives us many examples of how we can be holy by treating others with respect."

Esther recited the list, "Honor your father and mother, leave a corner of your field for the poor and the stranger, do not delay a worker's pay, do not curse the deaf or put a stumbling block in front of the blind . . . "

Mrs. Shapiro sat and smiled with pride at all that her students had learned. For once, she had nothing to add.

Now that you have heard what Esther and Danny have to say, make a list of things you want to say in your Bar or Bat Mitzvah speech. Who will you thank? From everything you have learned in the past few years, what do you want to teach the congregation?

PEOPLE I WANT TO THANK   **WHAT I'D LIKE TO TEACH**

_____   _____

_____   _____

_____   _____

Dictionary

מִלוֹן

	Chapter
א	
father	אָב
spring	אָבִיב
but	אֲבָל
love (masc. sing.)	אוֹהֵב
love (fem. pl.)	אוֹהֲבוֹת
love (masc. pl.)	אוֹהֲבִים
love (fem. sing.)	אוֹהֶבֶת
oy vey!	אוֹי וַאֲבוֹי לִי
eat (masc. sing.)	אוֹכֵל
_____ (4)	אוֹכְלוֹת
_____ (4)	אוֹכְלִים
eat (fem. sing.)	אוֹכֶלֶת
ears	אָזְנַיִם
brother	אָח
one (masc.)	אֶחָד
_____ (4)	אֶחָד אֶת הַשֵּׁנִי
sister	אָחוֹת
one (fem.)	אַחַת
there isn't	אֵין
Where?	אֵיפֹה?
food	אֹכֶל
mother	אֵם
_____ (6)	אָמֵן
truth	אֱמֶת
we	אֲנַחְנוּ
I	אֲנִי
dinner	אֲרוּחַת עֶרֶב
_____ (Intro)	אֲרוֹן הַקֹּדֶשׁ

	Chapter
land	אֶרֶץ
Land of Israel	אֶרֶץ יִשְׂרָאֵל
you (fem. sing.)	אַתְּ
you (masc. sing.)	אַתָּה
you (masc. pl.)	אַתֶּם
you (fem. pl.)	אַתֶּן
ב	
in	בְּ-
please	בְּבַקָשָׁה
_____ (Intro)	בִּימָה
between	בֵּין
hospital	בֵּית-חוֹלִים
synagogue	בֵּית-כְּנֶסֶת
Ancient Temple	בֵּית מִקְדָּשׁ
son	בֵּן
_____ (Intro)	בַּעַל-קְרִיאָה
morning	בֹּקֶר
daughter	בַּת
ג	
_____ (Intro)	גַּבַּאי
big (masc. sing.)	גָּדוֹל
big (fem. sing.)	גְּדוֹלָה
_____ (3)	גְּדוֹלוֹת
_____ (3)	גְּדוֹלִים
also	גַּם

Dictionary

מִלּוֹן

	Chapter			Chapter
		ד		
milk	חָלָב	sermon	דְּבַר תּוֹרָה
five	חָמֵשׁ	fish	דָּג
wedding canopy	חֻפָּה	uncle	דּוֹד
laws	חֻקִּים	aunt	דּוֹדָה
winter	חֹרֶף		
breastplate	חֹשֶׁן		**ה**
_____ (4)	חֲתֻנָּה	the	הַ-
_____ (4)	חָתָן	he	הוּא
		go, walk (masc. sing.)	הוֹלֵךְ
	ט	go, walk (fem. pl.)	הוֹלְכוֹת
good (masc. sing.)	טוֹב	go, walk (masc. pl.)	הוֹלְכִים
good (fem. sing)	טוֹבָה	go, walk (fem. sing.)	הוֹלֶכֶת
_____ (3)	טוֹבוֹת	she	הִיא
_____ (3)	טוֹבִים	today	הַיּוֹם
		they (masc.)	הֵם
	י	they (fem.)	הֵן
hand	יָד	_____ (3)	הַפְטָרָה
hands	יָדַיִם	_____ (Intro)	הַר סִינַי
birthday	יוֹם-הֻלֶּדֶת		
Thursday	יוֹם חֲמִישִׁי		**ו**
holiday	יוֹם טוֹב	and	וְ-
Sunday	יוֹם רִאשׁוֹן		
Wednesday	יוֹם רְבִיעִי		**ח**
Tuesday	יוֹם שְׁלִישִׁי	holiday	חַג
Monday	יוֹם שֵׁנִי	month	חֹדֶשׁ
Friday	יוֹם שִׁשִּׁי	sick (masc. sing.)	חוֹלֶה
wine	יַיִן	sick (fem. sing.)	חוֹלָה
boy	יֶלֶד	Cantor	חַזָּן

Dictionary / מִלּוֹן

Chapter		**Chapter**	
study (masc. pl.)	לוֹמְדִים	girl	יַלְדָּה
study (fem. sing.)	לוֹמֶדֶת	_____ (1)	יָפֶה
bread	לֶחֶם	_____ (1)	יָפָה
night	לַיְלָה	_____ (3)	יָפוֹת
to walk, to go	לָלֶכֶת	_____ (3)	יָפִים
to buy	לִקְנוֹת	there is	יֵשׁ
to read	לִקְרֹא	____ has/have	יֵשׁ לְ-
	מ		**כ**
from	מִ-	star	כּוֹכָב
what?	מַה?	cup	כּוֹס
_____ (7)	מוּסָף	cups	כּוֹסוֹת
water	מַיִם	write (masc. sing.)	כּוֹתֵב
letter	מִכְתָּב	_____ (4)	כּוֹתְבוֹת
king	מֶלֶךְ	_____ (4)	כּוֹתְבִים
_____ (7)	מִנְחָה	write (fem. sing.)	כּוֹתֶבֶת
10 adult Jews	מִנְיָן	all, every	כָּל
number	מִסְפָּר	dog	כֶּלֶב
_____ (7)	מַעֲרִיב	_____ (4)	כַּלָּה
commandment	מִצְוָה	yes	כֵּן
commandments	מִצְוֹת	crown	כֶּתֶר
Moses	מֹשֶׁה		**ל**
family	מִשְׁפָּחָה	to, for	לְ-
judgements	מִשְׁפָּטִים	no	לֹא
pray (masc. sing.)	מִתְפַּלֵּל	_____ (Intro)	לוּחוֹת
pray (fem. pl.)	מִתְפַּלְלוֹת	study (masc. sing.)	לוֹמֵד
pray (masc. pl.)	מִתְפַּלְלִים	study (fem. pl.)	לוֹמְדוֹת
pray (fem. sing.)	מִתְפַּלֶּלֶת		

Dictionary

מִלּוֹן

Chapter			**Chapter**		

English	Hebrew			Hebrew	English
do, make (masc. sing.)	עוֹשֶׂה		נ		
do, make (fem. sing.)	עוֹשָׂה		נָבִיא	prophet (masc.)	
_____ (4)	עוֹשׂוֹת		נְבִיאָה	prophet (fem.)	
_____ (4)	עוֹשִׂים		נְבִיאִים	_____ (3)	
_____ (4)	עוֹשִׂים חַיִּים		נוֹתֵן	give (masc. sing.)	
eyes	עֵינַיִם		נוֹתְנוֹת	_____ (4)	
on	עַל		נוֹתְנִים	_____ (4)	
next to	עַל-יַד		נוֹתֶנֶת	give (fem. sing.)	
_____ (Intro)	עָלֶיהָ		נֵר תָּמִיד	_____ (1)	
with	עִם				
tree	עֵץ		ס		
tree of life, Torah roller	עֵץ חַיִּים		סְכָרְיָה	_____ (3)	
evening	עֶרֶב		סוֹפֵר	scribe	
_____ (7)	עַרְבִית		סִפּוּר	story	
the 10 Commandments	עֲשֶׂרֶת הַדִּבְרוֹת		סֵפֶר תּוֹרָה	Torah scroll	
			סְפְרִיָּה	library	
פ			סְתָיו	autumn	
mouth	פֶּה				
Passover	פֶּסַח		ע		
_____ (1)	פָּרֶכֶת		עִבְרִית	Hebrew	
_____ (2)	פָּרָשָׁה		עוֹבֵד	work (masc. sing.)	
			עוֹבְדוֹת	work (fem. pl.)	
צ			עוֹבְדִים	work (masc. pl.)	
_____ (3)	צֶדֶק		עוֹבֶדֶת	work (fem. sing.)	
just or righteous actions	צְדָקָה		עוּגָה	_____ (3)	
noon	צָהֳרַיִם		עוֹלָם	world, universe	
			עוֹמֵד	stand (masc. sing.)	
			עוֹמֶדֶת	stand (fem. sing.)	

Dictionary

מִלּוֹן

Chapter	שׁ	Chapter	ק
seven	שֶׁבַע	sacred	קָדוֹשׁ
_____ (3)	שַׁבַּת חָתָן	marriage	קִדּוּשִׁין
hear (masc. sing.)	שׁוֹמֵעַ	read (masc. sing.)	קוֹרֵא
_____ (4)	שׁוֹמְעוֹת	read (fem. pl.)	קוֹרְאוֹת
_____ (4)	שׁוֹמְעִים	read (masc. pl.)	קוֹרְאִים
hear (fem. sing.)	שׁוֹמַעַת	read (fem. sing)	קוֹרֵאת
_____ (7)	שַׁחֲרִית	small (masc. sing.)	קָטָן
of, belonging to	שֶׁל	small (fem. sing.)	קְטַנָּה
hers	שֶׁלָּה	_____ (3)	קְטַנּוֹת
his	שֶׁלּוֹ	_____ (3)	קְטַנִּים
table	שֻׁלְחָן	summer	קַיִץ
my	שֶׁלִּי	parchment	קְלָף
yours (masc. sing.)	שֶׁלְךָ		
yours (fem. sing.)	שֶׁלָךְ		ר
_____ (5)	שֶׁלָּנוּ	head	רֹאשׁ
six	שֵׁשׁ	Rabbi	רַבִּי
two _____	_____ שְׁתֵּי	see (masc. sing.)	רוֹאֶה
		see (fem. sing.)	רוֹאָה
	ת	_____ (4)	רוֹאוֹת
thank you very much	תּוֹדָה רַבָּה	_____ (4)	רוֹאִים
under	תַּחַת	doctor (masc.)	רוֹפֵא
prayer	תְּפִלָּה	doctor (fem.)	רוֹפְאָה
Torah reading guide	תִּקּוּן לַקּוֹרְאִים	want (masc. sing.)	רוֹצֶה
nine	תֵּשַׁע	want (fem. sing.)	רוֹצָה
		_____ (4)	רוֹצוֹת
		_____ (4)	רוֹצִים
		pomegranate, Torah ornament	רִמּוֹן